GUIDANCE

for the Academically Talented Student

[Conference on Guidance for the Academically Talented ...]

Report of a Conference sponsored jointly by the American Personnel and Guidance Association

and

The National Education Association Project on the Academically Talented Student

Editor:

ELIZABETH M. DREWS **63716**
Associate Professor
Michigan State University
East Lansing, Michigan

Editing Committee:

CHARLES E. BISH
ELAINE COTLOVE
ARTHUR A. HITCHCOCK

National Education Association Project on the Academically Talented Student, 1201 Sixteenth Street, N.W., Washington 6, D.C.,

and

American Personnel and Guidance Association, 1605 New Hampshire Avenue, N.W., Washington 9, D.C.

Second Edition, omitting appendices

Any views expressed or recommendations
implied in this publication do not necessarily constitute official policy of the
Carnegie Corporation of New York, the
American Personnel and Guidance Association, or the National Education
Association.

This conference and report were made possible by
funds granted by Carnegie Corporation of New York.

Single copy, $1. Discounts on quantity orders:
10 percent on 2-9 copies and 20 percent on 10
or more copies. All orders which amount to
$2 must be accompanied by funds in payment.
Postage will be added to bills for orders not accompanied by funds. Address communications
and make checks payable to:

The American Personnel and Guidance Association
1605 New Hampshire Avenue, N.W.
Washington 9, D.C.

or

The National Education Association
1201 Sixteenth Street, N.W.
Washington 6, D.C.

CONTENTS

FOREWORD

At the greatest moments in the American past, Americans had an image before them of what free men, working together, could make of human life. The great question that the present generation of Americans will answer is whether the American democratic adventure can be continued and renewed and whether American life can be lit by a sense of opportunities to be seized and great things to be done.

These words, contained in the Rockefeller Special Studies Project Report VI, *The Power of the Democratic Idea,* characterize the tenor and substance of this publication, *Guidance for the Academically Talented Student.* The life and growth of the American ideal depends upon the development, in each child, of his desire to achieve his full potential, and upon the ability of his society to create opportunities which will make this achievement possible. In terms of elementary and secondary education, this means that all of our youth must have equal opportunities. Equal opportunity for those who are academically talented does not mean subjection to the same quality and quantity of educational experiences as are all others. Young people who are academically talented can be as thoroughly deprived by their educational experiences as students at any other level of ability.

A young person who has not had the opportunity to develop his potentialities adequately will find it difficult to choose his future in a setting of freedom. This problem is complicated by many factors. Some of these are set forth in the policy statement of the American Personnel and Guidance Association, issued December 12, 1957:

This generation has been called upon to make a decision that will shape the destinies of many future generations. At the heart of this decision lies one of this nation's basic freedoms—*freedom of choice.*

Faced by a tragic shortage of scientists and technologists we are strongly tempted to solve the manpower problem by channeling outstanding high school and college students into scientific and technical careers. Here lies the danger of tampering with freedom of choice. If the top academic potentiality of this nation were to be forced into a single selected career pattern, generations of youth

4

would lose the privilege of freely choosing their life careers—a privilege cherished by youth throughout the history of this nation. Such a course of action might not solve even part of the problem, for a lack of educated talent persists in all areas of our national life. The solution, therefore, must be viewed from a broader perspective, and we must aim toward utilizing every available talent. Only then will the demand for scientists and technologists be met, along with the demand for educated talent in all fields.

The present waste of human resources must be alleviated. It can be. This nation has an obligation to assure the maximum growth of all individuals, both for their own satisfaction and for the benefit of all society. With guidance, our youth can make their choices in freedom, and they can meet the human resources shortages in all areas of our democratic life.

The passage of the National Defense Education Act in 1958 gave voice to the national policy that opportunities be opened to the more able students and the point of view that the utilization of those opportunities rests, in large measure, upon the guidance function in education. This statement of national policy is put into practice each time a counselor works with individuals directly or indirectly. Faced by heavy demands, counselors in our schools are further pressed by a special necessity for conscientiously devoting to the more able student the same attention that is devoted to all others.

This publication contains both ideas for guidance work with the academically talented and specific ways in which these ideas can be actualized. It presupposes that the concept of guidance for the academically talented calls for a recognition of behavioral effects and the development of sound attitudes in individuals. Guidance personnel in our schools have a profound obligation to give particular attention to those who will furnish the leadership of this democratic society.

The guidance and counseling of academically talented students is predicated upon strong ongoing guidance programs. The school that wants to develop an individualized program for the guidance of talented youth must first provide guidance services for the entire school population. Within this established foundation, an enriched and specialized program of guidance and counseling for the academically talented can then be built.

The publication of this book, which we believe to be significant in education today, has been made possible through the combined efforts and talents of a number of people. The initial planning committee, consisting of Kenneth W. Lund, Chairman, Morris Krugman, and Merle M. Ohlsen, set the program into motion. Thirty-five persons, who convened in Washington, D. C., November 19-21, 1959, worked out an initial draft of the manuscript and reviewed the tentative draft during the ensuing months. Special appreciation is due to Elaine W. Cotlove for her valuable assistance. We wish to acknowledge particularly the work of Mary Clare Boroughs who devoted a great deal of time and effort to the production of this publication. Appreciation is also due Barbara Catton, Executive Secretary of the National Association of Women Deans and Counselors.

Special gratitude is due Elizabeth M. Drews, the editor, who responded so constructively to our request to edit the volume and whose contribution both to style and content made this volume possible.

On behalf of the American Personnel and Guidance Association, we wish to compliment Charles E. Bish, Director of the National Education Association Project on the Academically Talented Student, not only for his outstanding leadership in the area of guidance of the academically talented but also for his instrumental role in developing interest and projects in the area of education for the academically talented.

For the American Personnel and Guidance Association

Daniel D. Feder, President
Arthur A. Hitchcock, Executive Director

CONFERENCE PARTICIPANTS

Conference on Guidance for the Academically Talented Student
November 19-21, 1959

Steering Committee

KENNETH W. LUND, Chairman
Superintendent, Oak Park High School
Oak Park, Illinois

MORRIS KRUGMAN
Assistant Superintendent in Charge of Guidance
New York City Board of Education
Brooklyn, New York

MERLE M. OHLSEN
Professor of Education
University of Illinois
Urbana, Illinois

Conference Participants

WALTER B. BARBE
Professor of Education
University of Chattanooga
Chattanooga, Tennessee

HARRY O. BARRETT
Head of Guidance
North Toronto Collegiate Institute
Toronto, Ontario, Canada

R. S. BRACKMAN
Principal, Senior High School
Quincy, Illinois

PAUL F. BRANDWEIN
Senior Editor and Consultant to Schools
Harcourt, Brace and Company
New York, New York

LEO F. CAIN
Vice-President, San Francisco State College
San Francisco, California

ELAINE COTLOVE   Kensington, Maryland

NORMA E. CUTTS   New Haven State Teachers College
New Haven, Connecticut

ELIZABETH DREWS   Associate Professor
Michigan State University
East Lansing, Michigan

C. C. DUNSMOOR   Director, Board of Cooperative
Educational Services
Educational Services Center
Bedford Hills, New York

WARREN G. FINDLEY   Assistant Superintendent for
Pupil Personnel Services
Board of Education
Atlanta, Georgia

JOSEPH L. FRENCH   Assistant Professor
University of Missouri
Columbia, Missouri

JOHN C. GOWAN   Education Division
San Fernando Valley State College
Northridge, California

FERN HORNE   Director of Guidance
Mt. Lebanon High School
Pittsburgh, Pennsylvania

ROBERT B. HUGHES   Assistant Professor, School of
Education
University of North Carolina
Chapel Hill, North Carolina

BERNARD A. KAPLAN   Bureau of Guidance
State Department of Education
Albany, New York

PAUL R. KLOHR   Assistant Dean, College of
Education
Ohio State University
Columbus, Ohio

JACK KOUGH	Vice-President, Science Research Associates Chicago, Illinois
MORRIS KRUGMAN	Assistant Superintendent in Charge of Guidance New York City Board of Education Brooklyn, New York
KENNETH W. LUND	Superintendent, Oak Park High School Oak Park, Illinois
ROBERT D. MACCURDY	Professor of Education Head, Department of Education Centenary College of Louisiana Shreveport, Louisiana
WILLIAM H. MCCREARY	Chief, Bureau of Guidance State Department of Education Sacramento, California
ANNA R. MEEKS	Supervisor of Guidance Baltimore County Board of Education Towson, Maryland
LEONARD MILLER	Specialist, Counseling Techniques Office of Education Washington, District of Columbia
GLYN MORRIS	Director of Guidance Board of Cooperative Educational Services Lyons Falls, New York
ELIZABETH MORROW	Counselor, McKinley High School Washington, District of Columbia
KATE H. MUELLER	Professor of Education Indiana University Bloomington, Indiana

9

MARGARET O'BRIEN	Director of Educational Services Junior High Schools Evanston, Illinois
RICHARD Y. REED	Director of Guidance Workshop University of Miami Coral Gables, Florida
MAURINE E. ROSCH	Director, Guidance and Placement Cleveland Public Schools Board of Education Cleveland, Ohio
MILTON SCHWEBEL	Professor of Education College of Education New York University New York, New York
HELEN G. STERN	Counselor-Coordinator Nyack High School Nyack, New York
MARK M. TUCKER	Professor, Southwestern Campus Southern Illinois University East St. Louis, Illinois
H. DONALD WINBIGLER	President, National Association of Student Personnel Administrators Stanford University Stanford, California

CHAPTER 1

Identification

Academic talent is found in all social and economic levels of our society. In some instances, very able young people can be easily and quickly identified. Their zest for school and for learning, their life pattern of intelligent curiosity, and their high achievement in daily endeavors single them out as academically "top quality." These students receive scores of about 115 or over on a Stanford-Binet intelligence test, i.e., approximately one standard deviation above the mean, or they fall above a similar point on one of the Wechsler intelligence scales. They are the nation's finest students, that top 15 to 20 percent* of the high-school student body who are above average in learning ability and are considered to be good college material (8).

Within this group there is a much smaller portion—about 2 percent of the total high-school population—that is considered highly select. Students in this portion score 135 or better on the Stanford-Binet scales. The Stanford-Binet norms (5) set the precedent for them to be designated as "gifted," and they approximate, in intellectual level, the groups that others (1, 9) have termed "gifted." These students are the ones about whom there is public talk, writing, and argument. They are the subjects of a mounting array of research and literature. They are the children people hope will become tomorrow's "geniuses."

In this publication, discussion is centered around the larger group, which is designated as academically talented. It is evident that some of the principles and

---

* In more exact terms, 17 percent of the students are one standard deviation above the mean.

problems presented here apply more completely to the gifted student, with an IQ of 135, than to the able student, with an IQ of 115. In some instances, information has been drawn from research on the gifted and is identified as applicable to the top level only, or modified to include all of the talented.

In communities where education is not highly valued, where children are not encouraged to pursue academic interests, or where special populations affect the number of able children, less than 15 to 20 percent may be identifiable as academically talented. Communities such as university towns may contain more than this percentage. Each school administration must deal creatively with its atypical situation, but the over-all process of identification continues to be important in every situation.

Ideally, an identification program will make use of all appropriate available methods and persons in the school, the home, and the community. Intelligence and achievement tests are usually the means of screening for above-average ability, but occasionally school grades and observations of teachers, parents, and the children themselves are indicators of talents which tests may fail to reveal. The more complete the information a school has about each child, the more accurate the judgment of the ability of all children is likely to be and, at the same time, the less chance there is that a very able child will be overlooked.

WHAT TO LOOK FOR

Not all the traits indicating academic talent furnished in a printed list will be descriptive of any one child, and few children will have all of the qualities listed. Sometimes these qualities can be found in an average child, but a talented child will have more of them or have some of them to a greater degree. The items that

12

follow are intended only to give an indication of the traits to look for:

1. Early physical and mental development
2. Curiosity, alertness, observance, interest in many things, and a desire to be informed
3. Interest in books, especially reference books—dictionaries, encyclopedias, atlases—and biographies
4. Pursuit of an interest over a long period of time and with intense concentration
5. Easy and rapid learning
6. Reading, computing, and communicating with ease
7. Enjoyment of abstractions—generalization, making analogies, handling complexities, and using flexible, divergent approaches
8. Qualities of leadership and responsibility.

Those on school staffs know that each child has a different combination of intelligence, personality, and achievement and that one must be an astute observer if he is to detect all the above-average children in the school. An academically talented student may show superior competence in classroom work, extracurricular activities, and leadership; he may be outstanding in only one or a few areas; he may be underaged and physically smaller than his classmates; or he may be emotionally immature. Sometimes an average child may be mistakenly identified as superior. Several recorded illustrations of these various types follow.

A child like Bruce would leave no doubt that he is a superior youngster. He entered high school a year younger than his classmates, won eight letters in football, basketball, and track, was elected to the student council, and was on the honor roll each semester, even though he spent little time in study. He was very popular with boys and girls and was considered a leader by the faculty and students in his junior and senior years. His IQ score on a variety of tests was above 135 at each testing session. Bruce's observed achievements were consistent with the expectations derived from test scores and early accomplishments.

An example of the low achiever is Bruce's classmate, Jim, who was frequently in the principal's office because of unexcused absences and tardiness. He was impatient for the school day to end so that he could engage in a project of his own choosing—a project that frequently changed in content or purpose. His grades were average in most subjects and his homework was sloppy and often only partially completed. However, his insights in mathematics and biology were unusually mature and he was well informed on community and national affairs. Group intelligence and achievement tests in high school showed an IQ above 120 for him and achievement scores in the upper third of the national norm. Yet Jim rarely achieved the promise that scores predict in his traditional schoolwork.

There are times when the problem of identification is made even more difficult because some popular school leaders obtain above-average grades through hard work and personal charm rather than intellectual capability. Without tests, these students may be mistakenly identified as academically talented. Placed in situations where they must achieve at higher levels than they are capable of, psychological harm may result. One instance of this occurred in a community which instituted an accelerated reading program for those who were already reading considerably above the average of their group. As the group was charged with increased responsibility and more complex work, the teachers suddenly discovered that one of the girls was cheating. When group intelligence tests were administered that year for the first time, this girl was found to have an IQ of 109. Further investigation revealed that this was an accurate measure of her intellectual level. Apparently she had been achieving to the very limit of her ability before the speed-up program tempted her so much that she consistently cheated to retain her position as a high achiever.

With very bright children—those in the upper 2 percent of the high-school population—social, emotional, and physical maturity, although often above average, sometimes do not parallel intellectual development. Kathy illustrates this point. Upon entering kindergarten, Kathy was the youngest child in the room and was distressed when she realized that she was also the smallest child. When some classmates became six year olds, she cried because it would be so long until she was six. In kindergarten she earned a Stanford-Binet IQ of 141. Her reading and number readiness skills developed at a more rapid rate than those of most of her classmates, but her artwork was only average or below. Although at the close of her first day in the first grade she was upset because she could not read, she was soon reading at third-grade level. Now, in the third grade, she is below average in height and weight, yet she has an Otis IQ of 135, and her reading, arithmetic, and language scores are all fifth grade and above.

Robert's case is an example of the fact there is sometimes a great difference between intellectual and emotional growth. Even in the first grade his teachers considered him emotionally immature. In the first two years of school he progressed at an above-average rate in reading and arithmetic, but by the fourth grade he was being characterized as average by his teachers and test scores. His IQ, as recorded by a group test in Grade 3 was 95; a year later his measured achievement was still average in all areas on national and local norms. It was difficult to turn his attention to school tasks and equally difficult to hold it. The only clues (at first unrecognized) to superior talent were evidenced in athletic skill, in which he led his class, and in "do-it-yourself" projects where he progressed rapidly and attracted attention by building a crystal radio set. On the day his brother was born, he wrote a vulgar word on each of the first 135 pages of one of the school's books. Apprehended at page 136, he was later referred to a local child guidance clinic. A routine screening procedure used by the clinic included the WISC (Wechsler Intelligence Scale for Children), an individual intelligence test. His IQ was 123. Interpretation of this score surprised Robert, his parents, and his teachers. Once his ability was recognized and more effectively provided for, his achievement improved. The radio construction and athletic leadership should have suggested an individual examination, but his classroom performance had weighted the scales the other way.

It is apparent that children develop in complex ways. A teacher or counselor may even occasionally find that a general academic talent, previously unrecognized, can be identified by skillful performance in one area, such as English, mathematics, a foreign language, science, or social studies.

Although many academically talented students adjust well to school life, not all intellectually superior children are "ideal students." Some are nonconformists and refuse to "abide by the rules." They may be critical of school, teachers, and other pupils, unnecessarily absent from classes, may ignore instructions, fail to turn in homework, neglect details or be messy in their work, and may fail to conform in many other ways.

Sometimes signs of academic talent in boys and girls from low socioeconomic levels are not recognized. Unfavorable home conditions or neighborhood environment may obscure potential ability which exists but is not being disclosed by conventional tests and observation. This may also apply to children of religious and ethnic minorities.

Because so many factors must be considered in the discovery and evaluation of the academically talented, the most accurate appraisal can be obtained only by a thorough, systematic, and continuous approach and follow-up. Several persons, including the teacher, counselor, and other members of the pupil-personnel team, working together, will be more effective than one, but one person, usually the counselor, must be held responsible for an identification program. The next portion of this chapter discusses in detail how this can be accomplished.

PROCEDURES FOR IDENTIFYING THE ACADEMICALLY TALENTED

Identification procedures include the use of tests. In addition, observation by those in regular contact with able children—teachers, librarians, parents, classmates —can assist the counselor. Children's products in school and in extracurricular areas may be indicators of special talent. All pertinent information on an individual child should be kept in a useful form—the cumulative record.

Tests

In the search for academic talent, intelligence tests are necessary; many students have been incorrectly identified when this method has been omitted or has been inadequately used. Group intelligence tests usually are better predictors of success in the traditional school program than they are of general intelligence, for they are primarily measures of academic achievement. The individual intelligence test, which requires an examination period for each student, not only provides a more accurate intellectual appraisal, but also yields more information about each student examined than is possible with a group test.

The group intelligence test is necessary in any identification scheme, but the individual test is a very desirable component, even though it requires a trained psychological examiner and is expensive to use. During the individual testing session it is possible for the examiner to observe the student's reaction to a problem-solving situation and to study facets of the student's personality dynamics, as well as his intellectual functioning. The individual test is often used in conjunction with group tests. Usually a child should be given an individual test if he scores above 115 on a group test, if he scores considerably above his grade level on achievement tests, if he scores high on reading tests, if he has been singled out by teachers or peers as being particularly outstanding, or if he scores lower on the group tests than the experiences of the school indicate are consistent with his academic performance.*

If individual testing is not available to this extent, a series of group intelligence test scores for each individual will be better than only one. In any good testing program, a series of mental ability tests should be administered throughout the school years. If each student has three or more consistent test scores, recorded in different years, more reliance can be placed on the results. However, it must be remembered that scores from different tests may not be directly comparable and that all tests do not possess the same degree of reliability and validity. If a school system does not have its own services, outside agencies such as universities, child guidance clinics, counseling and guidance centers, state guidance personnel, and medical centers can sometimes offer assistance with individual testing and good advice on the choice of group tests.

Another test which will serve as a measurement of mental ability in the early grades is a reading readiness test. If a child consistently reads two grades above his level, this is a good indication of above-average intelligence. Schools generally begin to use learning aptitude and achievement tests in the middle elementary grades. The results, especially when they measure a

---

* Pegnato and Birch report that such an aproach is an efficient and effective screening procedure (6).

grade or more above the grade placement for a child of his age, help to single out the children with superior academic aptitude, as well as high achievement.

All tests must be sufficiently difficult to have an adequate ceiling. If any student can answer all the questions in a test, the test is inadequate. On the other hand, since practically all scholastic aptitude and achievement tests require a certain amount of reading ability, the academically talented student who is a poor reader will not be identified by this means. It must also be remembered that test taking demands a level head and calm emotions. Children who are poor readers, children who are slow starters and dawdlers, and disturbed children who are upset by the whole process make a poor showing.

The talented students from the lower socioeconomic levels may also have to be identified by other methods, such as those described by Kendrick (2) and Wright-stone (11).

Observation

Teacher. Since schools offer many opportunities for teachers to observe academically talented students, the teacher's role is an all-important one. He is the person who works with the student every day for many months. It is to him the student comes with his knowledge, abilities, problems, and queries. Thus, the teacher is in an advantageous position to identify the child with superior intellect.

In the early grades, the teacher usually knows how children vary. He knows the eager ones, the curious, the ones who seem to learn rapidly, and those who ask the most intelligent questions. The teacher might provide tests and games to bring out more of these qualities—informal quizzes or beginnings of stories for the children to complete. These are subjective means of identification, but they can be made more objective and useful if the teacher keeps a written record. Methods such as those suggested by Kough and De Haan (3, 4) may be used, or the teacher may create his own. Occasionally a creative and questioning child harasses a busy teacher, and, because he is not personable, he may not be accepted or recognized for his full intellectual ability. Therefore, whatever method of identification is used, it will be necessary for the teacher to be as unbiased toward the child as possible. If these observations are carefully recorded for each student, they can be the start of tangible identifying evidence.

Librarian. The school librarian has an opportunity to observe the choices of books made by various students and to take note of those who are reading above expectation for their age or grade level. Some talented boys and girls who may not care to achieve the best grades in school are recognizable by their avid intellectual reading. Students with reading difficulties may also show talent by searching for mature subject matter.

Parents. The school staff can sometimes gain leads to academically talented students by seeking the opinions and attitudes of parents. Too often school personnel are so busy telling the parents about the student that they do not pause to listen and to profit from the observations of the parents.

Students. Students are usually as well aware of the bright and dull children in each class as are teachers. In a class where students interact daily in a variety of situations, talent is hard to conceal. Simply asking, "Whom would you like to have help you with the schoolwork you missed?" or putting other similar sociometric questions to the class has helped to identify academically talented students.

Students' Products

Students' work should be studied for signs of creativity, originality, and interests that may be independent of the school curriculum. The intellectual content of artwork is an example. Autobiographies, written or presented verbally to the class, contain valuable information about children and also give indications of their facility in communication. The five-year study of the Portland, Oregon, program (7) outlines the city's plan for identifying and developing talent in creative writing. This plan, involving special testing and observation, could be used as a means of obtaining evidence of ability in self-expression.

Cumulative Record

To be of maximal help, the cumulative record should contain as much pertinent information about the child as it is possible and practicable to obtain. There will be standardized test scores, teachers' grades, records of attendance and citizenship, extracurricular and extra-school activities, the medical history, and data about the family. There should also be personal data collected by the school staff, such as observations pertaining to the student's interests, attitudes, and behavior in various activities. Anything that will help to give a clearer picture of the individual child should be included. For example, the outcome of parent-teacher-counselor conferences and anecdotal information may give clues to a child's performance. Conflicting evidence should be examined carefully. Contradictions between grades and test results, between present day-to-day behavior and behavior notes of the child's previous teachers, or a brief flash of talent where there is no previous record of talent should call for more intensive study of the student.

Persons who deal with pupils in an instructional or guidance relationship should help to prepare and should use such records. The preparation of adequate and suitable records requires the cooperation of teachers and guidance specialists alike, and, in the interest of uniformity and ease of interpretation, all must work together. In most secondary schools, the guidance specialist is responsible for the preparation and maintenance of records. In elementary schools that do not yet have adequate guidance assistance, the principal or teachers must assume full responsibility for the records.

The important thing is that adequate records be kept in every school and that they be both understood and used. The records must be started when the child enters school and maintained faithfully throughout the twelve grades. Adequately-kept records will disclose developmental patterns. With study and experience in the use of such records, it will become increasingly possible to utilize them in discovering academically talented students.

WHEN TO IDENTIFY

It is a common practice to delay the attempt to identify academically talented students until they enter junior or senior high school. Although it is important to identify them at that time, it is also important that they be identified before they have developed poor work habits or self-concepts that are not conducive to good academic work. Some students, by the time they reach junior or senior high school, may have already decided not to continue their education beyond the earliest possible school-leaving age and some may have placed irremovable ceilings upon their academic corridors. In addition, where early identification has taken place, the opportunity for enrichment of curriculum exists. It is, therefore, urgent that the identification process be started in the first years of elementary school —the first year is not too soon (10)—and that it be systematically continued throughout the child's school career.

THE ROLE OF THE COUNSELOR

The counselor has an opportunity to learn about pupils in many ways—through test results, records, conversations with teachers and other staff members, and interviews with parents and the pupils themselves. In order better to understand what is before him, the counselor, in cooperation with other guidance personnel, should form a plan for a general approach to identification, including the following elements:

1. Locate all school and community resources which might help in identifying talent. This means working with available personnel and includes the responsibility for encouraging identification as early as possible.

2. Where resources are inadequate, make needs known to the administrators. Explain what benefits further assistance would bring to the school, the community, and the academically talented child.

3. Organize a program for identification which is systematic and complete, so that meaningful records can be accumulated without loss of valuable time. The case conference, at which information can be pooled, should be part of such a program.

4. Work regularly with all school personnel to increase awareness of talent and to exchange information which might lead to identification.

5. Work with counselees to help them assess their abilities and limitations. As the counselor takes part in this continuing process, the needs of students will be revealed.

6. Seek to overcome any personal bias that could lead to overlooking talent. Talent is not limited to any social, religious, or economic group. The talented may be dirty, delinquent, and of various

religious faiths. Look for academic talent in all segments of the population.

PURPOSES OF IDENTIFICATION

This chapter, although devoted to the identification of the academically talented, has obviously and intentionally omitted discussion of the purposes of identification up to this point. Two major aims of adequate identification should now be stated. The first is the formation of a self-concept realistically linked to abilities. The second is the development of school programs which utilize and challenge academic talent.

Each child forms an idea, however vague, of his relationship to school on the first day that he attends kindergarten or first grade. This idea becomes more clearly defined as he goes through each day and year. The idea becomes part of what is appropriately termed his "self-concept." If he flounders in reading or arithmetic in an early grade, he adds this information to his view of himself. Other experiences during the school years increase his knowledge of himself, and each new experience solidifies more firmly his self-regard. Yet some or much of this information that he makes a part of himself may be erroneous. His failures in reading or arithmetic, for example, may not be caused by limited mental ability but by some other element that the alert school will be sure to help him to investigate.

The school must have, for its own use, the information about individual students that results from an effective program of identifying academic talent. But these identifying activities will largely be wasted unless the school consciously and conscientiously helps each of the academically talented students to understand himself more clearly—to form an honest self-concept. Robert's case is an example. His surprise at discovering something of his genuine talent could be duplicated in countless schools. It is possible, too, that Jim would have

CHAPTER II

Motivation

Motives are those needs and goals which incite men to action. They may also be defined as those social and psychological drives which move men to seek mastery of, or to allow themselves to be molded by, the people, forces, and institutions in their environment.

The better we are able to understand the needs and goals which nourish high achievement, the more intelligently we can act to motivate our talented children toward their fullest intellectual and creative productivity (5). The intellectual resources of our country are wasted prodigiously: approximately 50 percent of our college-capable youngsters never complete their college education; the majority of our academically talented females do not aspire to professional careers; and we are scarcely beginning to appreciate the untapped potential resources within our culturally and economically deprived classes. Our ever-accelerating rate of social and cultural change is also aggravating our manpower shortage.

Let us examine the nature and characteristics of the social and psychological factors which nourish or inhibit high achievement (20).

SOCIAL AND CULTURAL FACTORS

Each human infant is born with a unique genetic inheritance. That material from which his personality will develop is also present. The framework within which this development will take place will be determined, to a great extent, by influences found in his home, his school, and his society.

The Society

Our society predominantly measures an individual's success by "material" standards, not "intellectual" ones. We make conformity to the group the price of acceptance by the group. We are willing spectators and consumers of leadership; yet we are suspicious of the qualities and skills which make it effective. We conceive of knowledge as being basically utilitarian in purpose, not as an end in itself. Our cultural stereotypes of the scientist, the academician, and the artist as being anti-social, absent-minded, ineffectual, ragged, and amoral can only have disastrous effects. One study has shown that with this stereotype in mind, girls neither desire to become scientists nor to marry them (17).

There are many different cultural, national, and religious groups within our society, however, which hold more positive opinions regarding the nurturing of talent (10). Hopefully, some of our broadly prevalent patterns of anti-intellectualism seem now to be changing. As our leisure time and our wealth increase, unprecedented numbers of our citizens are finding time to develop their cultural appetites for books and records, concerts and art exhibits, home and foreign travel, and involvement and participation in programs of adult education. Certainly our access to the broad and varied experiences through which individual goals and values are developed and refined is vastly greater than before. Although there has been a definite increase in national concern about identifying and motivating talented individuals, changes in our cultural attitudes toward the intellectual, the nonconformist, and the creative individual, and attempts at understanding them, lag far behind.

The Home

The values and expectations of parents are those against which the child first measures himself. Numerous studies of the development of talent show that it

28

most frequently appears in homes where parents themselves are well educated and emphasize the "life of the mind (1)," or in homes in which parents themselves may not be highly educated, but nonetheless place a high value on education and learning. Such a simple measure as the number of books in a home has shown significant differences between high and low achievers (13). The development of talent is conspicuous among first-born and only children, whose early world is conditioned almost exclusively by adult figures and standards. The most important single factor in the decision of able students to go to college is the attitude of their parents toward higher education.

Parents can inhibit talent as well as nurture it. Inattention, criticism, ridicule, or hostility toward a youngster's efforts to explore ideas, to pursue special interests, or to achieve intellectual success can easily stifle a child's talent. The self-concept of the child whose early, none-too-perfect attempts to achieve are regarded as failures by his parents is, "I am a failure." For example, a third-grade boy who was repeatedly failing in his schoolwork was referred to a school diagnostician for an individual intelligence test. The test itself showed average ability, but throughout testing the boy kept repeating, "I'm dumb, aren't I?" It was learned that the child's father ridiculed him constantly at home. As the teacher emphasized to him day by day that she knew he was not "dumb" and that the test had shown this, as she kept repeating to him that she believed him capable of doing his work, there was a remarkable change in this boy's attitude. To achieve, every child needs an audience, however small, to appreciate and encourage his efforts. Parents are the earliest and most influential members of this audience (19).

The School

The school provides the child's first organized contact with a large group of children of similar age and diverse background. Here the values of the home are matched against and reflected in the mirror of society.

School experiences provide the boy or girl with an opportunity to grow in many ways: to learn new skills, to find new interests, and to acquire knowledge. When children are encouraged to move ahead at their own pace, they gain confidence and develop positive attitudes toward school. When they are discouraged by pressure to learn too fast for their ability, or where the educational process is one of boring repetition, negative attitudes may result. Thus, for the talented youngster, activities which use his more advanced abilities may be crucial in his motivation to achieve.

Within the boundaries of the school years, the talented young person is called upon to make decisions among a wide range of possibilities, all of which might, in one way or another, be called achievement-related. The preservation of his own sense of identity or individuality, the development of his own standards of performance, the formation of disciplined work habits, an orientation toward appropriately high future scholastic and career goals—these achievements may represent more difficult and less well-supported choices than the achievement of security through conformity by the adoption of the aims and values of the peer group (9). The educational program, the teacher, and the counselor play a key role in this selection of alternatives.

Culturally or Economically Deprived Groups

The superior student with a culturally or economically deprived background represents a special problem (3). Deterrents to his progress toward high academic achievement are: (a) low cultural values placed upon formal education; (b) lack of academic tradition in the family; (c) fear of parents that educational differences will separate the child from the family's sphere of influence; or (d) simple lack of recognition of intellectual

30

superiority. These, among other factors, may act to stifle or impede the student's acceptance of himself as a capable person, his ambition, his drive, and his consequent achievement. Low financial status and lack of information about sources of financial aid further represent an almost insurmountable barrier to the talented student's continued education. Frequently such students cannot be counseled apart from their family groups.

The evidence that such deprived students can be helped through concerted effort is presented by the project in Public School No. 43 (a junior high school) in New York City. The student body of this school includes many severely underprivileged children. Project students from that school placed 1, 4, and 8 at the time of graduation from a comprehensive senior high school, a record that had never before been achieved by students from that junior high school. It is also noteworthy that whereas 10 percent of the parents were initially involved, by the end of three years 90 percent were taking part in the program.

The Academically Talented Girl

By far the largest number of academically talented high-school graduates who fail to go on to college (up to 80 percent) are girls. A high proportion of the young women who do graduate from college fail to continue to work in fields in which they have received their education. It would appear, then, that there is a significant difference between the motivations of able men and of able women.

Our popular stereotype of the successful woman is the happy wife-mother. Our talented girls are persuaded that the twin careers of marriage and motherhood will continue indefinitely to enrich their lives, offering them the greatest possible development and fulfillment of which they are capable. The weight of our cultural emphasis converges on the feminine worlds of advertising, entertainment, fashion, beauty, and romance. This is an unrealistic picture in comparison to the worlds of professionalism, business, sports, travel, and politics which are unfolding before the talented high-school boy.

The academically talented girl faces a complex future in which her life will be revolutionized by higher and costlier standards of living, automation in the home, the development of service enterprises, and our exploding population with its attendant needs for more technical and professional manpower and womanpower. Her youngest child will be in school when she is still in her middle thirties, freeing an increasing portion of her time and energies. She probably will be able to satisfy her intellectual restlessness only in the world of work, frequently in hitherto masculine occupations.

The superior woman will carry a heavier burden than the superior man. If she wishes to combine the rearing of a family with work outside the home, she will not be content to do less than a good job with both. She will be competing for career opportunities against existing vocational prejudices and against talented men who are devoting their major energies to a life of professional advancement. She will also wish to be a helpmate to her husband and to encourage her children toward a richer personal development. Her double load is one of the unpleasant realities of our modern society, but it is one which can elicit from most of our talented young women a constructive and purposeful response.

Under the mores and attitudes of American society today, school girls will not be oriented toward work outside the home unless the public schools pay special attention to their motivation problems. The mass media give a disproportionate emphasis to romance and home life. The well-known phenomenon of cultural lag prevents young women from preparing adequately for careers. Social pressures to work catch up with women only in their thirties and forties, too late for adequate training. The counselor who would help the gifted school girl must not only be informed of her special hazards, but must also be open-minded and even adventuresome in his own thinking.*

PSYCHOLOGICAL FACTORS

Common factors in the psychological pattern of high achievement are high intelligence, specific talents, special interests, energy and drive, persistent effort, and self-discipline (14). A warm and basic acceptance by parents of the differences inherent in superior intelligence enables the bright child to develop a secure self-accepting concept of himself as a capable person and a worthy member of the family. The accepting family can respond constructively to the child's endless curiosity, his interest in words and ideas, and his urge to take part in activities unusual for his age. A strong self-concept provides him with a safe base from which to explore reality, to take risks as he attempts newer and more difficult tasks, to surmount repeated and inevitable failures, and to try again. The bright child is motivated to do this exploring and risk taking both by the high expectations of his parents and by his own inner developmental drives.

Through the setting and achieving of realistic but constantly forward-moving goals, the talented youngster gradually learns to adjust to the demands of the adult world. This may mean the postponement of immediate pleasures for future gains, development of responsibility for action, and critical analysis of choices and decisions with an estimate of outcomes. With adequate experience and guidance, the academically talented are able to learn these things sooner than average children. As these qualities develop, the talented student may learn to deal with frustrations in his life situation

---

* See footnote (4).

through concrete forward-moving action rather than by giving in to lesser values (15).

When the high achiever not only exhibits productivity in depth and scope, but also an unusual degree of originality, invention, and innovation, we call him "creative." Creativity occurs in every field of human endeavor.

What are some of the characteristics of creativity? Studies of highly creative people show that they have a high degree of tolerance for uncertainty, asymmetry, and ambiguity, that they enjoy the ordering of complex situations and resist early and simple solutions. They seem to be quite ruthless with themselves and even with others when they are intensely involved in the pursuit of an intellectual commitment, and they are insatiable in their thirst for knowledge, for variety, and for involvement in intellectual activities. For the highly creative person, a good part of his reward lies in the activity itself, rather than in the recognition which it inspires (2).

There will be some necessary and inevitable elements in the education of every academically talented youngster which act to inhibit productivity and originality. These include elements of the typical school program such as obedience to adult authority, restraints upon the free expression of feelings and opinions, rigid adherence to a set pattern or sequence of learning, deference to the needs and desires of the majority, lack of time and flexibility in the school day, and requirements to master certain subjects and skills in which there is little initial interest. In order to counterbalance these factors, the school must provide a greater proportion of positive motivating factors in the direction of high productivity and creativity. Encouragement and praise for academic achievement, intellectually stimulating curriculum content, the excitement of communicating with other equally able young minds, the contagion of the teacher's enthusiasm for his subject, high teacher expectations combined with an easy acceptance of occasional failures, opportunities for independent reading, research, and experimentation, the availability of an inspiring and scholarly adult with whom the student can identify—all these combine to strengthen the student's confidence in his choice of a difficult and challenging system of values.

Many talented adults can look back and identify one or several teachers who recognized and challenged their capabilities, fired their imaginations, and set them on the road to creative productivity. Gifted teachers attract and stimulate superior students. An additional important determinant in the development of a drive toward high achievement seems to be the experience, somewhere during the school years, that through his own individual efforts the able student can gain mastery of a field of knowledge, however small, and therein discover *by himself* new facts or relationships (18).

A number of questions of relative values remain unanswered. Is it really desirable, for example, for the highly creative student to achieve high academic standing in all academic courses? Although most academically talented students are multitalented and do almost everything well, some highly creative ones appear to be unidirectional. This may be due to an intense interest in a single area which draws time and energy from other activities. For example, a boy of considerable musical talent may be an active member of his school chorus, band, and orchestra as well as a private student in piano and the organist for his church. He may find that time for traditional schoolwork is limited and he is continually faced with decisions between working on vocabulary exercises or laboriously written Latin translations and practicing his music or even composing. If this highly creative student works hard to achieve success in his prescribed school subjects, will he thereby do violence to his special area of giftedness by depriving it of his time and energy?

In counseling with this type of student, it is necessary to consider the advantages of high academic standing in all areas and the advantages of the immediate development of special talents in relation to future goals. One student may choose to postpone some part of his creative efforts so that he may gain a variety of skills in a liberal arts college that requires a high grade point average. Another may elect to develop special talents with an eye toward specialized training and a career which may not call upon traditional skills. The role of the counselor is to help the student work through to an understanding of the alternatives of his action and his decision.

Where highly creative students are faced with such choices and where other talented students continually conform to work for good marks, the flexible school may seek to encourage creativity in both. Where achievement tests indicate that a student has already acquired skills, the wise teacher and administrator with a creative program can omit the usual assignments and alter some of the prescribed schedules to make room for suitable creative projects. In this way the problems of the creative student may at least partially be resolved, and other able students may also widen their horizons and gain access to creative and scholarly opportunities.

Is it desirable for the highly motivated able student to be "well adjusted" in the broadly conventional sense? Studies (18) indicate that the vocational choices of highly motivated and highly successful people are sometimes dictated by a socially constructive adaptation to a personal maladjustment: for example, the able individual in whom close interpersonal relationships produce anxiety can achieve excellence in the world of abstract and symbolic ideas, such as mathematics or science; the able individual in whom solitude and independence produce anxiety may achieve excellence in a field of social service. Would it be more desirable to try to alleviate these personal maladjustments, or to support the socially acceptable adaptations to them through which productivity can continue at a high level? Again, the answers are relative to the individual student.

The problem of "conformity" is a great one for the talented student. One point of view suggests that the talented student should not always be required to conform, but that he should be given help in knowing how to conform and how to be socially acceptable when the situation demands it.

PROBLEMS OF MOTIVATION IN UNDERACHIEVEMENT

The able underachiever is the student whose classroom performance falls far short of his capacities. This definition assumes that we are using teacher grades and performance tests as our criteria for achievement, not originality, productivity, or success in extracurricular pursuits. The pattern of underachievement in school, however, usually extends into, or is already to be found in other activities. This student may show little interest in school life and yet have inclinations toward originality and productivity, and apparent success in extracurricular pursuits. High achievement scores on performance tests are common for such students, in spite of low grades.

From 5 to 25 percent of the gifted students in many school systems are academic underachievers, and in some schools the incidence is higher. Contributing factors for which the school must assume responsibility are inadequate curriculum content, poor teaching, weak work habits and study skills, low academic expectations, lack of individual attention to students, and lack of intellectual stimulation and challenge. Within the school, these factors constitute the primary causes of underachievement among academically talented students.

Other factors in the school environment which may contribute to underachievement are excessive teacher authoritarianism, pressure to achieve in terms of the teacher's rather than the student's needs, emphasis on rote memorization rather than on analysis and understanding, suppression of intellectual controversy and of unresolved differences of opinion in the classroom, excessive competition for grades and honors, and contradictions between the values established in the counseling situation and the available curricular opportunities (16).

Academic underachievement is now regarded as a recognizable entity by the third, fourth, or fifth grade level, and is considered to be a "set" and relatively inaccessible pattern of behavior by the time the student enters high school. We do not know how early underachievement begins, but as we have indicated earlier, it would appear that in many cases its roots lie outside the schools, in early home and environmental influences.

Children derive their attitudes about themselves, for the most part, from the important and significant people around them: their peers, their parents, their teachers, and their counselors. Their concept of themselves as lovable, worthy of attention, capable of success, and secure in adult respect, is a reflection of the attitudes of the people with whom they closely interact. Unless the student has a great deal of self-initiated motivation and direction, he will need exposure to a source of motivation outside of himself to inspire him. Counselors and teachers should make every effort to find and expose their academically talented students to these motivating figures, either within or outside of the school environment (22).

Underachievers seem to come from families in which parents fail to see the child as a separate individual. These parents tend to act out upon him their needs, fears, and ambitions, as if he were an extension of themselves. Sometimes personal inadequacies may cause parents to regard the bright child as a threat and a competitor, someone to be "cut down to size." A common family pattern found in the homes of the underachiever seems to be the presence of a dominant and aggressive mother and a weak and ineffectual father (7). Parental overprotection rewards immature behavior patterns and penalizes independent thinking and activity. Excessive authoritarianism also inhibits the development of independence, and of assertiveness and spontaneity, particularly in the case of females. Excessive permissiveness, on the other hand, deprives the child of help in learning to control the expression of his primitive needs and emotions. This creates anxiety because it not only fails to define the boundaries beyond which a child's behavior is unacceptable, but also the boundaries *within* which he knows he is secure in adult approval.

As the insecure and anxious child proceeds within the school environment, new pressures and demands for conformity are added to his previous burden of conformity. The student already doubts his capacity to succeed, and when this inner doubt is reinforced by outer criticisms, failures, disciplinary actions, or peer group ostracism—some of which he unconsciously provokes—he retreats into negativism, passivity, or over-aggressiveness in the home or classroom.*

AGE AND ACHIEVEMENT

There is an important correlation between age and achievement. The age of peak quality of productivity for many highly talented people occurs not later than their twenties or early thirties, especially in the fields of mathematics, the physical sciences, and certain types of creative writing and musical composition. Career choices in these areas are not infrequently made during the high-school years. In the behavioral sciences, greatest productivity is likely to occur later.

---

* See footnotes (8, 11, 12, 21).

The academically talented young person who is highly motivated will often, nevertheless, be unable to achieve to his full capacity until he is adequately equipped with the knowledge, skills, and techniques of his subject choice. This consideration is important to those students for whom the opportunity to produce at a professional level is usually long delayed by intensive postgraduate, technical, or artistic training.

GUIDANCE AND COUNSELING IN THE MOTIVATION OF ACADEMICALLY TALENTED STUDENTS

The Home

Parents significantly influence the goal-setting behavior of their children. They can provide access to books, music, art, theater, museums, libraries, travel, political discussions, and knowledge of the customs and folklore of different cultural, national, and religious groups. They can provide a quiet place to study and help to budget time for study. They can encourage curiosity, intellectual pursuits, hobbies, and participation in adult interests. They can praise achievement for its own worth and refrain from measuring it by noncomparable adult standards. Then can inform and interpret to their children their special abilities and realistic vocational expectations. They can provide a family setting in which their children can safely express values and standards which are different from those of their peer groups. They can accept the fact that they are raising their children to lead independent and mature lives. Parents should allow the child to practice his independence as early and as frequently as their judgment and experience will permit. Parents must also recognize that high achievement is accompanied by many errors, mistakes, and failures, and should offer support and encouragement when the child becomes discouraged.

40

The School

A favorable pattern of the early school years and a favorable home situation are in many ways similar. The teacher should understand and be sensitive to the emotional climate in which bright children will be encouraged to put forth their best efforts. The teacher himself should be the kind of person with whom the child can communicate on a mutual level of intellectual awareness. He should be mature and well adjusted, so that he can consider the bright child objectively, regarding him as neither a threat nor an instrument through which to satisfy his own achievement needs.

The teacher can encourage early independence in thought and in action by providing many "open-ended" invitations to learning, problems in which more than one approach or solution is possible. He can also give approval to, and reward for, original thoughts and actions and encourage a classroom atmosphere in which individualism and a certain amount of nonconformity are regarded as acceptable behavior. He will, at the same time, indicate that acceptance and approval are not to be taken for granted, but are to be won by responsible and constructive social behavior. He will make plain his high academic expectations and his acceptance of mistakes and failures as a natural educational experience. He will apply discriminating pressure through the setting of high standards of achievement. He will make clear to his more able students that his different and higher expectations for them are not discriminatory but rather a personal recognition of their high potential and his way of honoring their individuality.

Incentives to challenge and develop the abilities of academically talented elementary- and secondary-school students can be provided by giving these students opportunities to use these abilities. This may be achieved through proper school placement, ability grouping in "clusters" or in subject areas, opportunities to explore in depth, under teacher guidance, certain aspects of a subject which are not covered in the regular course of study, independent "research" at an appropriate level, intensive accelerated programs, advanced college placement programs, and the opportunity to work with outstanding people in the community in their fields of technical or professional interest.

The school can assume the responsibility for maintaining a free exchange of information with the parents of academically talented students. School personnel can interpret to parents their information concerning test scores, teacher grades, and classroom performance; parents, in turn, can point out to the school important clues about the child which can lead to more adequate handling of special interests, abilities, and problems (6).

In a general school atmosphere of intellectuality and serious purpose, there is a greater likelihood that the able student will find intellectual goals worth seeking. He may rediscover the seeds of interest or discover new ones where none existed before. He can acquire desirable peer group status for academic excellence. It is hoped that his initial interest and pleasure in approval and reward for high achievement (a secondary motivation) may eventually be supplanted by an awareness of the sheer joy of learning (an enduring primary motivation).

The Counselor

The counselor plays a strategic role in the motivation of the academically talented student. He has had specialized professional preparation for, and experience with, the types of problems which the academically talented student will present. He is identified with this particular responsibility by the assignment which he holds on the school staff, and he is known to his stu-

(10)   Goldberg, M. L. "Motivation of the Gifted." *Education for the Gifted.* Fifty-Seventh Yearbook, Part II, National Society for the Study of Education. Chicago: University of Chicago Press, 1958. Chapter 5, p. 87-107.

(11)   Gowan, John C. "Dynamics of the Underachievement of Gifted Students." *Exceptional Children* 24: 98-101; November 1957.

(12)   Gowan, John C. "Factors of Underachievement in School and College." *Journal of Counseling Psychology* 7: 91-95; June 1960.

(13)   Hobbs, Nicholas. "Motivation to High Achievement." *Working with Superior Students: Theories and Practices.* (Edited by Bruce Shertzer.) Chicago: Science Research Associates, 1960. p. 247-64.

(14)   Lewis, W. D. "A Comparative Study of the Personalities, Interests and Home Backgrounds of Gifted Children of Superior and Inferior Educational Achievement." *Journal of Genetic Psychology* 59: 207-18; September 1941.

(15)   McClelland, David C., and others. *The Achievement Motive.* New York: Appleton-Century-Crofts, 1953. 384 p.

(16)   Mitchell, James V., Jr. "Goal-Setting Behavior as a Function of Self-Acceptance, Over- and Underachievement, and Related Personality Variables." *Journal of Educational Psychology* 50: 93-104; June 1959.

(17)   Riesman, David. "Permissiveness and Sex Roles." *Human Development Bulletin.* (Ninth annual symposium.) Chicago: University of Chicago Press, 1958. p. 1.

(18)   Roe, Anne. *The Making of a Scientist.* New York: Dodd, Mead & Co., 1953. 244 p.

(19)   Thistlethwaite, Donald L. "Effects of Social Recognition Upon the Educational Motivation of Talented Youth." *Journal of Educational Psychology* 50: 111-16; June 1959.

(20)   Tyler, L. E. "Studies on Motivation and Identification of Gifted Pupils." *Review of Educational Research* 27: 391-99; October 1957.

(21)   U.S. Department of Health, Education, and Welfare, Office of Education. *Guidance for the Underachiever with Superior Ability.* Bulletin to be published 1961. Washington, D.C.: Superintendent of Documents, Government Printing Office.

(22)   Wilson, Frank T. "Working with the Motives of Gifted Children." *Elementary School Journal* 57: 247-52; February 1957.

CHAPTER III

Education Provisions

Idealistically, the educational program of a public school should provide for the maximum intellectual growth of all students. The selective nature of this publication, however, necessitates limiting our discussion of the educational program to this question: What are the educational provisions which promote the maximum development of the academically talented student?

NEEDS OF ACADEMICALLY TALENTED STUDENTS

Personal Needs

Academically talented pupils have needs which are basic to all human beings: the need for security, for love, for belonging, and the need to be needed and to be accepted as an individual. Using Maslow's hierarchial classification, certain needs, such as needs for information, for understanding, for beauty, and for self-actualizing, might be termed higher-order needs (4). These are particularly important for the superior student. There is evidence that most of the lower-order needs are fairly well met for bright children. They are rarely hungry, relatively few come from broken homes, and most of them have interested and perhaps even devoted parents (5). However, the higher-order needs are not so easily met. A pupil who is obviously and sincerely engrossed in academic work, who seeks eagerly for information and tries to weave a pattern of the strands of knowledge, may be widening the gap between himself and pupils of average ability. A search for beauty or autonomy may be similarly misunderstood by other students and by teachers. One gifted tenth-grade girl was failed by her teacher when she gave the following definition of biology, "Biology is like beauty—it needs no explanation."

The problem of acceptance is a broad one, as will be shown in the chapter, "Counseling." It encompasses self-understanding and self-acceptance by the student as well as his understanding and toleration of the world in which he lives. Acceptance must also be viewed from the point of view of other pupils, teachers, counselors, administrators, and parents. Do these individuals accept the superior student, thus satisfying certain lower-order needs and making it possible for him to satisfy higher-order needs? Obviously, the most important kind of acceptance is a deeply personal one, one that colors speech and gestures and feelings. On another level of acceptance, counselors and other school personnel can take a number of concrete steps. They can take responsibility for identifying the academically talented. They can follow through on this by setting up desirable educational opportunities through courses, scheduling, and an adequate faculty. The counselors should be responsible for conferences about schedules, personal adjustment, and social relationships with others. The teacher's acceptance of the academically talented student is more apparent in the classroom situation and is of the utmost importance because it so often influences the acceptance patterns of the other pupils.

Acceptance by the teacher can take many forms, including respect for the talented student in all ways and regarding the able learner as a challenge instead of a threat. The teacher must remember that these pupils are still young and that although they are superior in knowledge to their peers, they need learning experiences and not apprenticeships as "assistant teachers." The teacher must maintain sound teacher-student relationships and prevent the additional adjustment problems which may arise if these superior students are established as "teacher's pets."

Self-acceptance and feelings of worth are basic to mental and psychological well-being. Young people characteristically develop such feelings of worth by doing a job well. There is a danger, however, in the present national search for able minds, that some capable and conscientious students will feel that "doing a job well is not good enough; only the superlative is acceptable." There is an accumulation of pressure for such students to take more academic subjects and to expend more effort and time in studying each subject in this expanded curriculum. Meanwhile, since pressures to be social, to be athletic, and to have outside interests do not diminish, the able student may very easily see himself as inadequate, for both he and all other human beings must, by their very humanness, fall short of such Olympian expectations.

Higher-order needs for information and understanding may not always be met easily by the school. Many students seek answers far beyond the limits of textbooks. A gifted first grader may plague his mother and teacher for an answer to the question, "How are A.C. and D.C. (alternating current and direct current) different?" A talented ninth grader may be eager to discuss theories of evolution. Counselors and teachers alike must encourage such quests for knowledge—here almost surely are the prototypic searchings of the creative scientist or scholar (1).

Appreciation of beauty in its many forms is also a need which the school may not have time or facilities to foster adequately. However, certain teachers with whom the student can study or meet on an extracurricular basis may have a deep sense of the original and the fine. Such teachers may encourage the talented students to produce in artistic areas, introduce them to museums, concerts, and fine books, and further their interest by arranging meetings with adult writers, artists, and musicians.

Finally, there is a need for self-actualization or autonomy. Maslow, in reporting his studies of self-actualizing adults, states that such self-actualization is a rare condition and that one seldom achieves it before the age of forty. However, superior students may be helped to move in the direction of actualization of potential capacities and talents, devotion to a mission or ideal in life, activity rather than resignation. As Maslow (1954) describes his self-actualizing people, they are "in general strongly focused on problems outside themselves"; they have "feeling for mankind . . . a genuine desire to help the human race . . . deeper and more profound interpersonal relations"; and they are "strongly ethical . . . have definite moral standards (4)." Obviously there is no easy route to such a goal, but satisfaction of lower-order needs may free the young person for further growth. Such growth can be stimulated by encouragement from counselors, teachers, and other adults (including artists, scholars, and scientists), as well as by exposure to models to emulate.

Educational Needs

There are certain needs of a general educational nature that counselors are accepting as common to superior children.* To a great extent these are extensions of the personal needs just discussed and especially of the higher-order needs. Listings of such needs usually include the following:

1. Development of independent study approaches
2. Acquisition of efficient learning techniques
3. Orientation in methods of research and problem solving
4. Development of special talents
5. Encouragement of creative thinking

---

* Many, of course, are needs of all children.

6. Emergence of human concerns (humanitarianism)
7. Development of communication skills.

It is debatable whether or not able young people feel these as needs, but they are qualities seen by adults as desirable for both the general social good and for the individual good. An educated person has a need for compassion and a need for competence. Such competence is far broader than excellent daily recitations or near-perfect examination papers based on a textbook. It includes an ability to seek out knowledge and learn when there are no blueprints such as workbooks or assignment sheets. It assumes skills in problem selection, hypothesis forming, data collection and evaluation, and synthesis or concluding.

Over and above these abilities are the more creative ones and those related to talent development. Methods and techniques can be taught; creativity must be fostered. Creativity has been defined as knowing what everyone else knows and seeing what no one else sees. In the arts, it is a search for beauty; in the sciences, a search for truth. Students may need to be helped here in order to find time for "creative solitude" or to organize their lives in such a way that there are extended periods for writing, practicing, or painting.

All of these needs point to the fact that adequate educational provisions must allow the able pupil to become an individual. He must not be shaped into a pseudo scholar who simply parrots information or an automaton who conforms because he has not been taught to think for himself. Some of the needs are means; others are ends achieved from those means. Obviously, learning techniques, research methods, and problem-solving methods are merely aids in the development of an independent and/or creative scholar.

Independence in scholarship is a need often ignored by our schools. The very presence of a daily assignment acts as a deterrent for the development of scholastic freedom. One young teacher, concerned about the monotony of daily assignments and the uninspired quality of students' work, deliberately sought to develop independence in her classes. After a survey of literature was presented in her ninth-grade English class, opportunity was given to the students to read in depth or breadth in individual areas of interest which had arisen as a result of the preceding literature unit. No specific type of literature, author, or topic was assigned.

For two or three days the students insisted upon being told what to do, but by the end of that time nearly everyone had explored library material to the extent that he had found some area of interest with which to begin. Most became deeply engrossed in their topics as their research progressed; some found that their interest had waned, or that an interesting facet they had uncovered had led to another area of reading. Typical projects included the following: "Women Poets of America," "The Works of Poe," "New England Poets," "War Stories and Poems," and selected readings in drama, biography, and short stories. These are some of the comments made by the pupils:

"It gave me a wonderful opportunity to read whatever I wanted . . . . In most classes I would never have a chance to do that."

"It led to new interest . . . ."

"I had not had the chance before to do something like this . . . ."

"I think I have read more since we started this project than I have in all the rest of my life put together."

". . . This is only the beginning of research for me because I have only touched a small pinhead of what there is to be had in books."

THE EDUCATIONAL PROGRAM

The framework in which this kind of teaching occurs needs to include, for the academically talented pupil, a core of subjects in the basic areas of English, mathematics, science, social studies, and foreign language. These courses are generally included in the college preparatory sequence in the high school, thus attracting the academically talented group. Adequate programs of identification and guidance further assure the homogeneity of these classes and encourage all able students to participate in this program. Also, information concerning the range and direction of ability and the number of pupils involved becomes pertinent for class content, sequence, completeness of sequence of the classes in these basic areas, and number and types of elective courses to be offered.

It is not enough, however, merely to include those courses generally thought to satisfy college entrance requirements. This practice does not take into consideration the quality of learning experience offered to the pupil. Studies have clearly indicated that there may be great divergence of learning from school to school or even from teacher to teacher where the same curriculum is used. Such divergence is indicative of qualitative variations. An adequate program must, therefore, provide more than an adequate course of study. It must include teachers who have a knowledge of their subject area, who are skilled in teaching techniques, and who are familiar with able students. It must also include adequate materials. Communication with parents and community is another integral part of an ideal program.

Although the responsibility for the educational program rests ultimately with the adults of a community, the school administrators are primarily responsible for its presence, direction, and ultimate success. They must realize that the development of a program which meets both personal and educational needs and which stresses quality rather than unending and repetitive quantity requires, along with the approaches mentioned, teachers of a special nature and adequate materials.

52

Research studies on teacher quality have not been conclusive. However, there are in the literature descriptions of outstanding teachers which reveal certain universal qualities (2). Teachers of able students must themselves be able scholars. It has been said, "You can no more teach what you don't know than you can come back from a place you haven't been." This means that a teacher must have knowledge of his subject, enthusiasm for it *as a subject,* and an obvious curiosity to learn more about it. The teacher must instill into the student not only a love of the subject, but also a love of learning and a knowledge of the learning skills.

Perhaps a word of warning is needed here. Enthusiasm for the subject and love of learning are necessary, but if these qualities are misguided or lacking in direction, much effort will be lost. The teacher must not only know his subject, but his pupils as well. This comes primarily through the identification program, but also through a genuine interest in the pupils and their interests. The teacher must be prepared to recognize that bright ninth-grade pupils are no longer at the ninth-grade level in most areas. The old saying, "Take the children as you find them and carry them as far as they can go," was never more applicable than when one is working with capable students. Nothing so deadens their interest in a subject and their desire to learn as drill on material they already know.

Superior students who are achieving close to their level of ability function well in the classroom if they have concise examples, experiences at their level of understanding, enough drill to establish learning skills, and, finally, a project which they can successfully carry to completion through the use of these skills. They are eager to learn new things; they want to use their school time to the best advantage (3). They should be given opportunity for discussion and exchange of ideas. Because their minds grasp connotations and new concepts easily, they enjoy exploring the thoughts of others and forming opinions as a result of discussion.

The teacher should not assume that the able student is equally capable in all areas of study. If he checks on relatively simple material occasionally and, in addition, takes care to establish rapport with his students so that they feel free to ask questions, these unexplored pockets of learning can be filled easily in a minimum of time.

Materials can do much to supplement good teaching. An adequate supply of source materials should be provided for a wide range of subject matter areas. The opportunity to study in depth must also be provided. Even very young gifted children have interests far beyond the home, family, and community emphasis found in the basal readers. Some are fascinated by prehistoric animals. (One little boy was a specialist on whales.) First graders sometimes do not have library privileges, yet recently, in one school where most of the first graders were reading books at fourth- or fifth-grade level, there was a wholesale consumption of trade books by the end of the year. One girl read 60 books above and beyond the basal series.

Junior high-school students may have similar problems in obtaining appropriate material for their special projects or more esoteric reading interests. Adults' books, especially those of a specialized nature, are not commonly found on the shelves of the intermediate level libraries. Special provisions must often be made for students to use city and state library facilities, and the counselor who is aware of these student needs can be most helpful in making such arrangements.

Much has been said about utilizing multiple sources of information in the classroom. Of course! One cannot prepare a feast of learning with a dearth of materials. The teacher faced with a heterogeneous group is often almost appalled by his responsibility to provide material for the learning levels he finds in the class. Varied learning levels are also present, to a lesser degree, in a so-called homogeneous class. If this homogeneous class is on the upper level, the reason for providing a variety and quantity of material is different. In this case, materials are not provided because of anyone's inability to read and comprehend, but for the purpose of broadening the pupils' insight into the problem at hand. The teacher must take primary responsibility for judicious choice of the materials, particularly at the beginning of study. He is equally responsible for developing the pupils' own abilities to be selective with references and to base their opinions of the merits of various sources on sound and objective thinking.

The role of the teacher should be one of guidance, not direction. This shift of responsibility for judging references to the student is only one method the teacher should employ. He should use, at various times, all the teaching methods at his command, never losing sight of the fact that his primary concern is with teaching the techniques of learning. No one can learn for the student; he must do this for himself. Learning—writing, talking, exploring, listening, thinking, or meditating—is an active, not a passive process. Active participation does not necessarily mean noise; the right kind of silence is also productive. The necessary criteria for learning is that the activity, either oral or silent, be alive!

Naturally, mistakes are going to be made in this type of permissive atmosphere. The teacher must school himself to accept this fact and must realize that error often provides the rich soil of experience. Many pupils have been made to feel that they should always be right, and this feeling creates its own problems. Everyone should have the right to make mistakes, even the superior students!

A program which includes teachers, materials, and methods thus geared to the needs of able students should satisfy the needs of most of the academically talented. However, in individual cases, teachers or counselors may find students who are not satisfied. These may be the highly gifted who are insufficiently challenged, the unilaterally talented who seek more opportunity for self-expression in a particular area, or perhaps the able but not highly gifted in this broad grouping who find the competition too keen. When a student does not feel challenged, it is the responsibility of adult personnel to confer and to adjust the student's program in terms of his special needs.

Many ideas for enriching educational experience will be found in the listing in Appendix A.

RESPONSIBILITY OF THE GUIDANCE SERVICES

The guidance services are discussed at length in another chapter. However, the role of the counselor in the educational program can be further emphasized at this point. Obviously, if the school is to schedule realistically for talented students, and if teachers are to teach in the best possible way, information on pupils must be complete and comprehensible.

Guidance personnel have a major responsibility for providing this complete information for administrative decisions and for assisting teachers in working effectively with such students. For the files of each class, the counselor can compile lists which indicate the range of abilities of students and approximate numbers within these ranges. This information should be presented in a way that insures maximum efficiency in class and classroom grouping.

Further information should be readily accessible to teachers. This would include data indicating special talents which the teacher can encourage and utilize and information pertaining to skill deficiencies which enables the teacher to strengthen weaknesses quickly and prevent future difficulties. The counselor should help to interpret the student to the teacher. When a student is achieving below his potential, it is important that the teacher know the actual discrepancy between ability and achievement and thus be prepared to challenge the unused potential.

In addition to preparing adequate student records, the counselor is in a position to work with administration and teachers on curriculum development. Although superior students rarely fall below grade level in classwork, they need special material at a higher level as well as further variety which may be introduced to meet a broad range of intellectual interests. In the current press for more scientists, the counselor may play an important role by influencing the development of programs in other areas, such as the creative arts and social sciences.

In addition to these specific services to administrators and teachers, the counselor has certain responsibilities in counseling the superior student in educational areas. This includes responsibilities for opening up enriching opportunities for students outside of the classroom. Many communities have programs in art, science, and other areas which give the able student an opportunity for expansion. If these are available, the counselor should help the student to participate in them. If they are not available, the counselor might well be the person who arouses interest in developing such programs. Appendix B contains an annotated list of programs in various subject matter areas. The counselor is encouraged to promote the use of this list for aids and examples in building up such activities. This list is broad in geographical coverage and rich in variety of academic interests.

Where students have been identified as academically talented and offered a particular program, their attitudes toward themselves, schoolmates, teachers, and schoolwork may be affected. The guidance counselor can do much to avert possible problems.

One such problem is the need to develop appropriate modesty. As long as the pupil conceives of learning as "how much I know," instead of seeing it as a process in which he continually confronts the unknown, the problem of self-centeredness will exist. Once the student recognizes the vastness of the infinite unknown, this problem may solve itself. This attitude can often be achieved in counseling sessions as well as through the challenge and competition of a class of talented students.

Another phase of modesty exists in relation to the high standards these pupils hold for themselves. It is difficult for the typical "C" student to appreciate the fact that a "B" for these bright boys and girls may represent failure. The superior students can save themselves unpopularity by holding back their fears and distress before and after grades are received on tests or report cards.

Another related problem area for these students also lies in their standards for themselves. Many of them, because they are acutely aware of quality, strive for more than time or energy or their current abilities permit. This pressured attitude is often encouraged by teachers who seek to inspire their students to unrealistic heights. At times the counselor may be needed to help superior students understand themselves and thereby temper their high expectancies.

In heterogeneous classes and in social contacts, superior students are generally the most active participants. Teachers and counselors alike can seek to train these boys and girls to contribute in such a way that their ideas are understandable and enlightening. The development of this ability to "translate" is particularly crucial for the very gifted if they are to make the mark on society that their talents promise.

Finally, since the superior student is alert and creative in many areas, it is often difficult for him to accept the need for drill and discipline in basic skills. These students need to recognize that great talent is almost always exhibited in forms learned through intensive study. For example, if they aspire to write well, such basics as spelling, handwriting, and vocabulary drill come first. Further discipline needs to be encouraged in the thinking process itself. The mind that can produce a ready answer to every question must be trained toward self-criticism and the rethinking of first impulses. The counselor will meet many an impatient bright student.

In all of these areas the counselor can contribute, through the counseling sessions, to the personality development and social adjustment of the academically talented, as well as to their educational growth. The need for such help may be particularly pressing for the more highly gifted who feel estranged and are over-critical of school and the learning process.

SUMMARY

In order to meet the needs of academically talented students, educational provisions must be made. College preparatory courses are not sufficient. High-quality teachers and curriculum materials, as well as an atmosphere that encourages accelerated development, are necessary factors, too. The counselor contributes to this phase of a school program by providing accurate information on students' abilities and interests and by handling special problems in personal development that arise among academically talented students.

REFERENCES AND BIBLIOGRAPHY

(1)   Brandwein, Paul F. *The Gifted Student as Future Scientist.* New York: Harcourt, Brace & Co., 1955. 107 p.
(2)   French, Joseph L., editor. *Educating the Gifted.* New York: Henry Holt & Co., 1959. 555 p.
(3)   Hechinger, Fred M. "Summer Rebellion." *New York Times,* August 14, 1960. Section 4, p. 8.
(4)   Maslow, A. H. *Motivation and Personality.* New York: Harpers & Brothers, 1954. 411 p.
(5)   Terman, L. M., and others. *The Gifted Child Grows Up.* Genetic Studies of Genius, Vol. 4. Stanford, Calif.: Stanford University Press, 1947. 448 p.

CHAPTER IV

Counseling the Academically Talented Student

Guidance principles permeate the total educational program when there is widespread commitment to individual freedom and responsibility and a firm respect for individual differences. This means that most of the directions will come from within the counselees. Therefore, counselors and other school personnel must be sensitive to these directions and administrative policies flexible enough to allow for their development. Such a guidance climate may exist when there is little or no formal guidance program, but it is more apt to prevail when there is a competent guidance staff and when such principles have become a vital part of the school's philosophy, objectives, instructional practices, and special services.

Counseling the academically talented is predicated upon the understanding that the school has a sound guidance program that benefits all students. The goals for counseling are several. There is an obligation to help the able individual develop more completely in human areas, not only as a fully functioning individual with a strong sense of self-worth, but also as a person who has compassion for others, a desire to contribute to society, and a willingness to take responsibility. There is a need to foster his intellectual growth, to broaden his educational and cultural experience, and to develop a taste for learning as its own means and end. Finally, there is the need to open routes for him to explore and enhance his areas of interest and have confidence that these explorations will help him find his way to wise decisions.

There are certain qualities of mental superiority—and problems which relate to this superiority—that make special demands upon the school and especially upon the counselor of the academically talented student. Some of these qualities, such as early mental and physical development, broad interests, and a desire for stimulation, have been mentioned in Chapter I, "Identification." The problems and needs that these qualities may produce will be included in this chapter. Specifically, the following pages will cover: (1) Guidance Personnel; (2) The Counseling Process, with emphasis on (a) social and emotional problems, (b) vocational aspirations, and (c) educational concerns and plans; and (3) Parental Factors and Home Environment as they affect counseling.

GUIDANCE PERSONNEL

The amalgam of successful guidance programs is undoubtedly a balanced formula derived from relationships and attitudes of the people who are involved in their operation. The guidance services, if they are to be effective and if they are to produce a guidance climate, come from the cooperation of many different people— a positive interaction that is basic to an effective program. It is unlikely that an individual counselor would have the time or the competence to assume all of the guidance *action*. Even if he did, there would be an unhealthy thinness in this climate. The counselor, however, is the one who will take *responsibility* to ensure that the guidance aspects of the total program for the academically talented are well met. There must be a clear point of responsibility.

The following section is concerned with the roles of the school staff members who are usually the most active contributors to the actual guidance process. These include: (a) the counselor; (b) the school psychologist; (c) the psychological examiner; and (d) the social worker. They, in turn, work with teachers, administrators, and parents, as well as with the students themselves.

While the roles and educational preparation for these four professional areas may differ, the attributes which make them particularly suited for work with the academically talented do not. In addition to an empathy with all young people, those who work with bright students must be able to enjoy them and their gifts without feeling threatened by intelligence which may exceed their own. Such staff members should also appreciate the quest for truth and have an affinity for scholarship which makes it possible for them to listen with interest to esoteric conversations of the highly gifted and to recognize the areas of conflict and special needs of all these students.*

The School Counselor

Responsibilities. In the complexity of the modern school system, the school counselor has two basic responsibilities with regard to talented students. His primary responsibility to the individual student is to aid him in self-understanding and acceptance, as well as in charting an educational and vocational course. With this goes the additional responsibility to work with others who deal with these students—teachers, administrators, parents, and the community-at-large—and to guide them in their understanding of the able student as they help him to responsible citizenship.

There are many specific ways in which a counselor can fulfill his task. He may be able to provide information on classroom materials. He may have specific duties in the school testing program. He will counsel the students on both routine matters and more complex adjustment problems. At all times he will be working with the other guidance personnel, as well as with resources in the community.

---

* See footnote (4).

Because they are vital to the academic needs of superior students, suitable materials are often a basic concern of teachers. The counselor, with his knowledge of vocational information which is aimed at high-level ability and describes challenging professions, can help the teachers. In addition, provision for books and pamphlets which give insight into the behavior of these students can benefit both teachers and administrators. It may be that the counselor can tap community resources, such as civic groups, to finance the purchase of these materials.

The guidance staff of a school is usually responsible for the selection and administration of psychological tests. This responsibility includes arranging for tests of achievement and aptitude, as well as for more detailed individual testing. Since tests for the academically talented may differ from those routinely administered, the counselor needs special knowledge in this area.

In counseling with individual students, routine matters such as curriculum plans and future education will frequently be discussed. There may also be problems of general adjustment between teacher and student which the counselor can interpret and help to resolve. For example, it may be difficult for a teacher or an administrator to understand why John, with an IQ of 130, turns in smudged papers filled with misspelled words and framed with crooked margins. It may be difficult for John to understand that legible, clean, and accurate papers, papers which invite rather than repel readers, are important if he wants to become a scholar and to communicate with others. The counselor can, perhaps, explain to the faculty that John's behavior is not atypical of rather bright boys. He can then help John to understand the need for clearer and more careful exposition. Thus, the counselor may achieve a degree of rapprochement between students and staff.

The counselor will also meet more complex adjustment problems among superior students. He must realize that when Mary, a science talent winner, repeatedly shows evidence of emotional instability, it is his responsibility to call in the school psychologist or other mental health workers. In such a case, further consultation with the school social worker could lead to referral to community services. In situations of this nature, the counselor stands as a bridge between the student and the services needed for long-term treatment.

Professional Preparation. In order to perform these functions with the academically talented student, the counselor should have professional training in psychology, sociology, and education. He needs special skills in person-to-person counseling, as well as the ability to meet many segments of the public. While the people currently working in this area come from a variety of backgrounds, there is agreement regarding the professional certification of counseling personnel. At a conference on the identification and guidance of gifted children, held under the auspices of the American Association for the Advancement of Science, the following recommendations (1, 2) were made:

1. Minimal: the master's degree in a program of counselor preparation which includes a core of study in psychology and education and some supervised experience in counseling.
2. Desirable: a two-year graduate program including considerable practice and internship.
3. Optimal: the doctorate in a program of counselor preparation which fully encompasses skills and knowledge in such areas as educational and psychological tests and measurements; interviewing; referral techniques; occupational information and counseling skills; knowledge of personality psychology; handling students and their problems; knowledge of social institutions in education and industry; broad background in behavioral and social sciences; knowledge of American educational philosophy; specific psychological skills.

In addition, the current study of guidance in American schools, under the sponsorship of the American Personnel and Guidance Association, is expected to evolve a broad outline for the education of counselors for American schools in the next several decades.

There are also opportunities for inservice training. Some special sessions are arranged for the counseling staff of a large school; others for all counselors in a smaller system; and still others are offered on a state or national level (such as the National Defense Education Act Guidance and Counseling Training Institutes). At such meetings there are opportunities for all guidance specialists to meet together, so that counselors, psychologists, social workers, and others can share knowledge. The psychologist may contribute to an understanding of therapy from the clinical point of view. The social worker can provide new insights into case history development or methods of interviewing parents. Personnel directors and placement officers may be called upon to supplement the counselor's knowledge of available occupations in this changing world. Special sessions dealing with superior students can be arranged.

In addition, meetings of guidance staff can provide opportunities for acquiring and refurbishing skills, for developing new attitudes toward young people, and for gaining fresh insights into their problems. Educational films on the counseling process and role playing, and analysis of recorded interviews do more to facilitate learning than abstract discussions.*

The School Psychologist

Responsibilities. The school psychologist in the larger school systems serves primarily as a director of testing programs and as a resource leader for remedial services (such as reading and speech), social case workers, and school counselors. The psychologist may also be called upon to offer special assistance in arranging for the

---

* See footnote (7).

curriculum and for teacher preparation in special classes, including classes for superior children. In addition, the psychologist has been trained in research methodology and is particularly qualified to conduct educational research or to advise staff members on research projects.

Training. Certification as a school psychologist generally necessitates a doctorate in clinical or educational psychology. This training includes a period of internship in school as well as in community mental health services.

The Psychological Examiner

Responsibilities. In the smaller system, the school psychologist may also serve as a diagnostician. There are, however, personnel whose primary function, under the supervision of the psychologist, is a diagnostic one. The diagnostician, or psychological examiner, is usually responsible for the administration of individual tests to students referred to him. In the case of superior students, this includes standard intelligence tests as well as additional tests of ability and personality, especially in cases of adjustment difficulty. The diagnostician is expected to present coherent reports of his findings and recommendations to the referral source—administrator, teacher, counselor, or social worker.

Training. The training for a diagnostician is similar to that of the psychologist but is more limited. It includes rather thorough training in test construction, administration, analysis, and interpretation. The master's degree should qualify a diagnostician for the administration and interpretation of individual and group tests.

The School Social Worker

Responsibilities. In some systems, school social workers are a part of the guidance staff. They are known also as "visiting teachers," and "visiting counselors." The social worker's orientation leans toward environmental effects on the individual. Therefore, the social worker naturally deals with parents and the community, as they influence the child. In their work, school social workers deal primarily with parent-school and parent-child or teacher-child relationships.

Training. Social workers are expected to hold the master's degree. Their training should include supervised case work in school situations.

THE COUNSELING PROCESS

The principles of guidance and counseling have been stated in the introduction to the book and to this chapter. The fundamental concern is with the right of the individual to make his own decisions, whether they are of a personal, educational, or vocational nature. Thus guidance becomes a matter of helping the individual to identify variables relevant to his situation and to arrive at the best weights for each of the variables in the equation of choice. The process is concerned not only with the more obvious variables of aptitudes, interest, and job opportunities, but also with the myriad subtle inclinations, likes and dislikes, apprehensions, and aspirations. The best kind of guidance develops in the counselee an attitude of problem solving and an ability to follow through in decision making. Typically, counseling involves two individuals—the counselor and the student—in a face-to-face relationship in which the student, his plans, concerns, and problems are considered. It allows the student to gain a better understanding of himself and to relate this understanding to a better understanding of the world around him. The two desired results of counseling, therefore, are a tentative determination of direction and a more facile skill in being self-directive and in handling problems.

There are many techniques and approaches used in counseling. Some are more suitable for personal counseling and others for educational and vocational counseling. Some appear more appropriate for certain students and others seem better suited to the temperament and thinking of a given counselor. Generally speaking, counselors tend to be client-centered or directive or some combination of the two. Most are not inclined or appropriately trained to use psychoanalytic procedures.

Client-centered counseling rests upon the doctrine that counseling consists of helping the student to mobilize his own resources in the solution of his own problems. This is accomplished by an attitude of acceptance on the counselor's part and by nondirective procedure. The counselor seeks to understand the counselee's own terms or frame of reference. Directive counseling is the procedure in which a counselor attempts to control, directly or indirectly, the areas discussed in an interview, by describing the choices which confront the student counselee and/or offering specific advice.

Those qualities in academically talented students which appear to stem from their ability to think intelligently produce an early ability to investigate many matters for themselves and to arrive at wise decisions. Furthermore, because of their independence they usually resist adult attempts to control their thinking in any way. Therefore, the client-centered approach is more suitable in work with able boys and girls. This becomes increasingly evident in the discussion that follows.

Three dimensions of counseling will be considered here: (a) personal-social effectiveness or competence; (b) career planning or choice; and (c) educational adjustment and planning. Of course, this does not mean that these areas are mutually exclusive or that it is possible to label students' problems that easily. Nevertheless, counselors sometimes find it convenient to speak of counseling in these three dimensions.

Personal-Social Counseling

Counseling which is directed toward helping the student grow emotionally and socially in a healthy, positive direction demands an atmosphere of warm human relationships. The counselor must realize that such positive growth results from adequate learning of new responses on the part of the student, learning which is facilitated by an appropriate counseling climate. Such a climate develops when the counselor genuinely likes and accepts students, feels them worth his time and effort, and, finally, shows his ability to empathize—an attitude of understanding and acceptance, of an unstated "I know how you feel."

In his contacts with able students, the counselor must ask himself, "How can I best produce the kind of atmosphere that will be nonthreatening and stimulating, a climate that will encourage positive growth?" These students particularly flourish when treated on an equalitarian basis. They may resent adults who preach and give ready answers. In reporting on class sessions and group therapy approaches that they have liked, talented students made such comments as these:

"I particularly liked being treated as an adult."

"It was good to be in a group where we all felt comfortable."

"I liked finding an adult who would listen and try to understand."

Such a counseling philosophy means that the counselor of the superior student does not try to explain that student to himself, nor does he outline a credo for living.

1. Counseling Problems

Perfectionism. The superior student may find that his needs for supremacy and top performance become so great that he will not chance a so-so performance in academic, athletic, or even social events. In some cases this may result in withdrawal from threatening situations; in others, in a mounting tension over failure to meet self-styled standards. This problem may alienate the superior student from classmates who do not hold such high goals for themselves and who cannot fathom such fears and dissatisfactions.

Love of argument (8). Parents rarely complain that their able offspring are combative in a physical sense, but parents and teachers alike are sometimes annoyed by their love of argument and dissent, and by the fact that, "at the top of their voices," these students are so often right. On the face of it, this may not seem to be a problem for the students, but since adults, in their own insecurity, may need to feel supreme, problems often do result. Able and overly expressive youngsters prove to be irritating and are rejected by the very group—the meaningful adults—to which they have made a bid for acceptance.

Immodesty. Often young people also take exception to argumentative and "know-it-all" ways and feel that these pupils with the knowledge and well-filled minds lack proper modesty. Part of their rejection may stem from the fact that superior students do not have patience or time to translate their ideas. They find it easier to speak in the jargon that they read than to translate and interpret. When asked to help with schoolwork, they more often do it themselves than explain it adequately. As Leta Hollingsworth noted long ago, the gifted need "to suffer fools gladly."

Less pronounced interest differences between sexes. It is true among superior boys and girls, as it is among gifted men and women, that there are less pronounced sex differences with regard to interests (10). The able boys may be interested in art, literature, and music (traditionally feminine interests), as well as mathematics and science. Able girls may be fascinated by rockets and jets and the binomial theorem, as well as humanistic studies. A studious, well-informed boy is sometimes called a "sissy," while a girl who learns eagerly

70

and speaks authoritatively runs the danger of being tagged "mannish."

These four problems are illustrative of the problems* encountered in counseling with academically talented boys and girls. With all four, as with other problems which may be related to superior intelligence, the degree to which they are present varies not only with individuals, but also with the level of intelligence. Whereas the students with IQ's of 115-120 might feel less pressure in these areas, those with IQ's of 130 and above can hardly escape these stresses brought on by their talent.

2. Counseling Methods

There are certain characteristics of the counseling process, if it is to be more than a single meeting of student and counselor, that are barometers of progress or of improved self-perceptions. Typically, it is difficult for the bright student with a personal problem to get to the heart of the matter immediately. It may be less threatening for a bright girl to talk about external matters such as a poor grade in gym, than a personal concern like her feeling that "knowing the answers" and "being a bookworm" may keep boys away from her door forever.

Counselors often find it desirable to find out about students' interests and hobbies before the counseling sessions and to plan for a conversation that will help the student talk easily. For example, Jack, a bright boy who made model planes, was finding it difficult to discuss the impending divorce of his parents. By discussing a current magazine article on model planes, the counselor helped Jack to begin to talk about his interests and home life. Thus the counseling process can lead from the external and objective to the internal and subjective, to areas of intimate revelations (which the counselor should not force).

---

* It must be remembered that there are other problems which arise out of the school and family setting, such as pressures from school and parents and conflict between desires for peer acceptance and performance that excels.

In a satisfactory counseling experience, the counselee often moves from a tendency to overgeneralize and think in terms of "black-and-white" to a more realistic view of the situation. Occasionally, a student will be deeply despondent, as was sixteen-year-old Sam, the brain in Physics II. He burst into the counselor's office and stormed, "No one cares if I live or die. All they want to do is pick my brains. If I can help them translate Ovid—fine—but no one will talk to me like a person!" Gradually, after several sessions, Sam came to understand that the problem was not that simple. It was not true that everyone rejected him—Bill had made overtures just last week—and Sam could begin to see that sometimes he rejected others before they could know him. Such movement toward reality, the separation of the solvable problems from the overwhelming general dilemma, is an aspect of positive growth.

The successful counseling process should also help the counselee move from a negative, hopeless attitude about himself toward a more positive view. Judy, an attractive superior student, was insecure in social situations. She expressed her fears by saying, "I'd rather just stay in the library where no one can see me." The counselor and teachers together were able to help Judy recognize her assets—intelligence, artistic ability, and physical charm. By working with other students on posters and magazine illustrations, she was able to forget herself and start on the road to social poise.

In counseling in this area, the counselor may well be called upon to bring other personnel, aside from classroom teachers, into the process. Where parents and home environment are involved, the school social worker may be able to play an effective role. Students who appear to have more severe adjustment problems should have the services of the school diagnostician or psychologist to determine the depth of disturbance. In such cases, referral to guidance services outside the school may be necessary.

72

3. Counseling Outcome

The intelligence of the superior student can serve him as well in the counseling process as in the classroom. He has many qualities which help him develop better attitudes toward himself. Studies (3, 5) have shown that superior students typically possess more independence, goal orientation, reality concept, mastery of environment, and problem-solving ability than average students. These are the very qualities that such psychologists as Jahoda, Maslow, and Brewster Smith have used to describe the mature and well-adjusted individual. These are the qualities which assist the superior counselee in making routine decisions and in meeting problems requiring more radical adjustments.

Counselors who have made a practice of working with academically talented students have reported rewarding experiences. Superior students, according to experienced counselors, have a facility for reaching a richness of insight that less able students may never find. This insight, which the counselor seeks to encourage in the counseling process, is essential to superior students in the unfolding of relationships and the self-understanding that constitute both the material for solving problems and the bases for developmental programs ahead.

As a result of successful counseling, the counselor will have the satisfaction of watching the superior students develop a sense of self-worth and self-direction. He will see these young people opening up to the possibilities for intellectual challenge and social responsibility that lie before them. He will see them freed from inner fears and inhibitions, able to consider many possibilities, make realistic decisions, and form warm personal relationships with confidence.

Vocational Counseling

In addition to counseling in the personal-social area, the counselor's primary concern must be the career growth of the young person. In the process of vocational counseling, as in all counseling, he must genuinely believe that the counselee, with self-understanding and appropriate information, can make sound choices and plans. It is implied that each talented student has certain abilities, interests, and predispositions which, when he becomes aware of them and pursues their development, will make him a contented, self-reliant, and effective citizen.

1. Counseling Problems

Awareness of interests and talents. Bright boys and girls have wider interests and greater talents than average students. Because of this, a selection of an interest for lifetime emphasis may be more difficult for them. Everywhere they look, they see challenge and feel equal to it. In addition, early school experiences may not be broad enough to touch on areas of greatest specific ability for an individual student. Superior students need to be aware of their assets and yet be prepared to change their goals if a new area is opened to them.

Motivation to high goals. Gifted boys and girls are qualified to seek high goals and to succeed. Not only national need, but their own personal needs for self-fulfillment urge that these young people be motivated to search out opportunities that will utilize their full potential. Whereas superior boys often do aspire to high-level occupations, superior girls appear to need special encouragement. Particularly in cases where family plans and aspirations do not challenge superior students sufficiently, the school carries a responsibility for motivation.

Need for information. Motivation without information is worthless. Superior boys and girls need to know what professions are available to utilize their talents. They also need to be aware of the training required and the time and cost (financial, personal, and social) that may be involved.

Need for models (5). It is particularly difficult for superior students who come from nonprofessional homes to visualize themselves in higher level careers. Since increasing numbers of academically talented students have this need, provision of models—local and national professional men and women—is an important area for development. This can be done through visiting speakers and encouragement of special contacts outside of school through part-time work in selected settings or attendance at cultural events where outstanding individuals are featured.

2. Counseling Methods

Adequate vocational counseling, like other good counseling, permits the greatest degree of ego involvement on the part of the student. The student must feel a concern about careers and must ask questions before any "supplying-of-answers" will be effective. In other words, readiness for career planning is as important for the academically talented as for others.

Counseling can best proceed after the stage is set—when the student has an interest and has begun to ask questions. Obviously the counselor can help this to happen. At this point, student and counselor together can gather information and weigh it against the student's abilities and interests. Out of this a tentative decision may result. Prior to college such decisions usually will be general ones—in an area or at a level— rather than exacting specifications for a narrowly defined occupation.

The case of Roger clarifies several points about individual development through counseling. Roger and his high-school counselor framed an interesting and challenging program of studies that would enable him to enter college at an advanced level in some course sequences. Roger felt strongly directed toward a career in teaching speech and dramatics, but the counselor encouraged him to keep the future open. Together they investigated many career possibilities.

During the summer before college registration, Roger met with his college counselor. At that time a liberal arts program was planned without commitment to a major. After several interviews the counselor noted that social sciences would be a distinct possibility for Roger, with career prospects in government, politics, foreign service or foreign enterprise—goals commensurate with Roger's talents. At this point Roger had to reach some decisions about his values in life. The counselor conferred with Roger a number of times during the first two years in college and less frequently, but regularly, thereafter. Roger sought continually to clarify his goals, but he was beset by many interests. The counselor did not force Roger, but tried in different ways to help him see himself and his future more clearly. At the time of this publication, the young man has completed his doctorate in political science, has had a year as a Fulbright scholar which the counselor helped him plan, and is studying to enter the diplomatic service.

Roger is an example of the able student who seeks for some years, spanning high school and college, to find the point of focus amid his many talents. The process of vocational counseling is made somewhat easier than it may appear in this case by the fact that superior students may have explored vocations earlier, tend to view them more realistically, and are better able to understand the full array of openings and the endless demands of training processes and higher education.

In counseling with superior students, the counselor serves as a source of information on career possibilities. The counselor must be aware that many of the occupations which will exist in 1970 are still unknown today. This means, however, that he can help the student to become aware of the great social and economic needs of the coming decades—for teachers, for economists, for city planners, for atomic specialists—and he can create an awareness of the exacting and changing world in which people will work in the student's adulthood.

The temptation to try to mechanically match measured talents with work requirements is ever-present. With the academically talented this can be very easy because some collection of measured aptitudes is certain to fit the requirements of some occupational field that appears reasonable. This stereotype of vocational counseling of an earlier period is most inadequate for superior students. Because it fails to involve the student directly in the process of decision, this method is likely to fail in producing the flexibility and inner drive necessary for the achievement of complex goals.

While the counselor endeavors to assist the student in recognizing his potential capabilities and in charting possible careers, he is not a sales promoter. In fact, the counselor may need to help students separate helpful information from propaganda designed to entice them into special areas. The momentary temptation to give in to the persuasive methods of certain professional groups can be resisted intelligently if the superior student is sufficiently informed about and self-confident of his goals.

Counselors may also find that students need to explore the world of work. Direct contact with an occupation through part-time jobs may be best, although interest may also be aroused by interviews with effective adults in appropriate careers and by selected reading. Biographies often prove inspiring to able students and key figures may become models.

3. Counseling Outcome

The counselor's role with the academically talented student, relative to his career life, is primarily to help him acquire a sound concept of himself. It is the entire person that eventually enters a career, not a segment of talent. Everyone acquires some self-concept. With the help of appropriate guidance services, beginning in the earliest school years, the concept that the academically talented student builds about himself can be thoroughly sound and substantial for life-long growth by the time he is in senior high school. This concept will and should change during the years of career life, but if a sound core has grown during the school years, the individual can readily make modifications in accordance with new experiences.

The second part of the role of the counselor in vocational counseling is to help the academically talented student widen his horizons to the varied possibilities that his talents indicate. Rapid changes in economic career life today make it unwise to seek any narrowly construed objective. Rather, the counselor must help keep career paths wide and open-ended, encouraging educational planning and career goals that recognize human adaptability of the able to the changes of a fast-moving economic and career pattern. That human adaptability is conditioned by the help of the counselor in facilitating wise planning.

Educational Counseling

Educational counseling is primarily concerned with problems that emerge in the school and whose solutions will, in turn, affect school progress or functioning. Many of the suggestions in the chapter on "Education Provisions" refer to ways in which the counselor can help work out a better educational program and superior educational plans with the student. However, certain problems such as achievement, school attendance, school activities, short-term educational plans and choice of courses, and long-range educational objectives, were not discussed. Educational counseling would thus take place with bright students who are low achievers or potential dropouts, with those who are uncertain about extracurricular participation or who partake in too little or too much of it, with bright students who must decide on a program (college preparatory or other) or on electives, and with those who are preparing to select a college.

1. Counseling Problems

Low achievement. Some students of potential academic talent do not achieve to the expected degree in school. They do merely fair work; a small percentage may fail time and again, in spite of evidence seen in intelligence test scores, previous records, or daily classwork. This problem is more frequent among boys who, even at the top level, are outnumbered 2 to 1 by girls in grade point average. The problem of low achievement is elaborated in Chapter II. Lack of motivation may stem from boredom with traditional curriculum, inadequate personal goals, or more deep-seated emotional disturbance. While low achievement may not always be indicative of future performance, high-school grades are still the best predictor of college success; so the matter is worth considerable attention.

School dropout. School dropout is a particular problem for superior students if their potential is to be developed. Almost a decade ago Wolfle stated that the dropout rate of superior high-school students between high school and college was approximately 50 percent. Current estimates of dropout percentages are smaller. For example, two recent state-wide surveys (Wisconsin and Indiana) of dropout rates of superior students showed that 65 to 85 percent of the boys in the top 10 to 25 percent of the student body were planning to attend college. More of the equally able girls were dropping out—only 45 to 65 percent were planning to attend college.

Extracurricular activities. Extracurricular participation plays a large part in the school life of most superior students. Many surveys and research reports have shown that they participate in more activities of all kinds than other students and that they are especially active in music and art programs and organizations such as science and chess clubs. They hold more offices in student organizations than other students.

Course selection. Selection of courses is not an easy problem for superior students who are eager to learn many things and who are often aware that careers of the future may take on such new dimensions that today's academic routines are already outdated. Course selection problems can also develop because of students' aversions or preferences for teachers.

Future educational plans. College selection is an important undertaking for the able student. For the most gifted, all colleges that offer appropriate courses will be possibilities if fees and distances are not prohibitive. For a student who stands at the eighty-fifth percentile, a college with very high admission standards may be an unwise choice. There are more than 2000 four-year colleges and universities in the country and over 600 technical schools and two-year junior colleges. Somewhere within the limits of the schools that admit almost any high-school graduates and the colleges with rigorous academic standards will be institutions that are appropriate for the students in question.

2. Counseling Methods

The counselor is basically responsible for the academic progress and plans of his counselees. Such matters as low achievement, school dropout, extracurricular activities, and course selection should be routinely investigated and discussed. For example, the counselor's folder should include information on extracurricular participation. Where it is obvious that a student has taken on too much or too little, the counselor may then make a special effort to discuss planning of time with the student. Sometimes activities can snowball to a point where schoolwork suffers or the routines of living, such as eating and sleeping, must be too rigorously curtailed. In a few cases students may fail to utilize extracurricular opportunities to broaden their interests and experiences.

In some cases where special difficulties are encountered, assistance from other staff members may be needed. For example, John, a boy of considerable mathematical talent, was failing regularly in history and English. Since his file did not contain evidence of an individual intelligence test, the counselor first made a referral to the school diagnostician. When an IQ of 125 was reported, the counselor talked to John at length about his school problems. Since the boy showed signs of anxiety about his home and family life, the school social worker was called in to determine his home situation. The social worker made several visits to John's home. As family tensions eased, John's marks improved somewhat. Arrangements were also made for some special help for John in areas of weakness stemming from the early grades. However, years of inadequate work in certain areas, as well as unresolved family difficulties, continued to handicap this boy. It was the counselor's opinion that if John's symptoms and problems had been detected and analyzed in the elementary grades, guidance for both the boy and his family would have proved effective.

As the counselor guides students in the selection of high-school courses and in the investigation of career opportunities, he must also inform them of the training requirements in the careers under consideration. For superior students, college training is basic to any realistically challenging career, but in the case of the students with highest potential in the academically talented group, the possibility of graduate study should also be considered. Therefore, the counselor must be well acquainted with information on colleges and universities— their standards, requirements, particular assets, and their personalities.

To aid a student in college selection, the counselor needs to consider not only the interests and abilities of the student, but also the financial status of the student and his family. Honest discussion in this area may lead to the investigation of scholarships and work opportunities as well as to consideration of the less expensive institutions suitable to the student's goals.

The high-school counselor is responsible for directing students to the specialized tests for college aptitude and to scholarship testing programs. The National Merit Scholarship Tests which attempt to select the most intellectually able should be considered. There are also advanced level batteries in mathematics and science and specialized tests such as those measuring aptitude for medicine, law, engineering, or nursing. The superior student is likely to do well on many tests. Any decisions here, as in all areas, are decisions the student must make for himself.

As the counselor progresses with a student toward college choice, visits to the campus or personal interviews with college personnel should be arranged. The counselor should know about and share information with the counselee on such programs as early admissions and advanced placement. The Advanced Placement Tests of the College Entrance Examination Board serve an important purpose in permitting academically talented students to progress to more suitable, advanced courses in college on admission, and may, at the same time, enable them to save a semester or more along the line of study required for the professions.

When a choice has been made, the counselor prepares a transcript. It is important that this present a clear and composite picture of the student, honestly stated. This is one of the first sources of information from secondary school to college and its importance cannot be overemphasized. Many admissions officers feel that the high-school counselor is the one person at the secondary-school level who really knows the student and is best able to evaluate him objectively and professionally.

In a recent panel of academically talented high-school seniors and college freshmen, students expressed the unanimous feeling that high schools should send, and colleges accept in the same setting, much more information about the students. They expressed the wish that more information would be transferred—and assimilated—about them as persons with doubts, hopes, values, and aims. They wanted to go from high school to college without a frustrating waste of time while they were "relearned."

The counselor can do much to protect his counselees from the pressures of alumni groups, staff members, parents, and community. It is a rare college that fails to proselyte the most able students in some manner. Superior students may also encounter teachers who are eager for them to follow in their footsteps. Janet, a highly gifted girl, now a university major in psychology, was urged by her ninth-grade art teacher to concentrate in art and was offered free art lessons; in the tenth grade her music teacher discovered unusual talent and arranged for her to have free flute lessons at the university; and in the eleventh grade she was encouraged to enroll in a university statistics course which resulted in research in programing for an electric computer!

3. Counseling Outcome

Counseling with students of superior ability in the educational area should result in the best possible use of their talents while in school. The counselor may help encourage low achievers and those who plan to leave school too soon. He may seek to help students balance their academic and extracurricular programs and assist in planning courses that suit their abilities.

Furthermore, successful educational counseling in high school will direct students to colleges and universities that offer courses to meet the student's goals, with sufficient challenge for those who are most gifted. In educational counseling, as well as in personal-social and vocational counseling, high-school and college counselors guide the academically talented boys and girls along paths that will provide an opportunity for self-fulfillment and offer the best of their talents to the service of society.

PARENTAL FACTORS AND THE HOME ENVIRONMENT

Recent factors concerned with motivation, academic achievement, and personality development have made counselors much more aware of the importance of the home. Such concerns are explored at greater length in the chapter on "Motivation." Certain factors, however, are of such importance that it seems wise to re-emphasize them at this point. Implicit throughout personal-social, vocational, and educational counseling is a need to work cooperatively with parents.

The importance of the home environment has been particularly emphasized in two recent reports of long-term studies with able children. Sontag (6, 9), Director of the Fels Research Institute, points out that students who typically rise in intelligence (he calls them "risers") come from homes where they receive both encouragement and freedom. Similar findings are reported by Bowman (3), Director of the Quincy Youth Development Project, who notes that able, high achievers come from homes where there is much communication and mutual understanding and where parents provide a wealth of experiences—music lessons, dance, visits to museums, etc. It is becoming increasingly apparent that parents can do much to cultivate talent and to enhance motivation.

A true need exists to work closely with parents on all levels of counseling with students—kindergarten through graduate education. In the case of academically talented boys and girls, it may be possible to work with parents as a group, informing them of the school's program and goals and of the possibilities for their children in future education. Records of parent attendance at such meetings should be present in the student's file, as well as adequate records of other contacts under various circumstances. The counselor who listens carefully can usually learn much about the home from the student's spontaneous comments. Students often convey the attitudes and aspirations of their parents.

At times it may become evident that special problems exist in the home. The counselor may learn that parents do not recognize or encourage the ability of their child, that parents disagree in viewpoint, or perhaps that they expect too much and exert undue pressures. When these problems arise, the counselor should request that a parent or parents meet at the school with him, or perhaps with several staff members, to discuss the student and his needs. If such an appointment indicates a need for further contacts, the social worker may be called in to continue with the case. Particularly in planning for college, parents need to be informed on the decisions that are being made.

SUMMARY

The academically talented student, like all students, needs to become a fully functioning individual, able to meet the demands of his future with assurance. The guidance staff—counselor, psychologist, diagnostician, and social worker—is responsible for serving the particular needs of able students in the areas of personal-social, vocational, and educational development. Through contacts with parents and students, adequate guidance can assure that the high potential of these students is actualized—for their good and for the benefit of the community in which they live.

REFERENCES AND BIBLIOGRAPHY

(1)   American Association for the Advancement of Science. *Identification and Guidance of Able Students.* Report of Conferences on Testing and Counseling. Washington, D.C.: the Association, 1958. 32 p.

(2)   American Personnel and Guidance Association. "Professional Training, Licensing and Certification." *Personnel and Guidance Journal* 37: 162-66; October 1958.

(3)   Bowman, Paul. *Education of the Gifted*. A paper delivered at the American Psychological Association Meeting. Chicago: September 1960.

(4)   Council of Chief State School Officers. *Responsibilities of State Departments of Education for Pupil Personnel Services*. Washington, D. C.: the Council, 1960. p. 25.

(5)   Drews, Elizabeth Monroe. A *Four-Year Study of 150 Gifted Adolescents*. Report to the American Association for the Advancement of Science. Washington, D. C.: December 1957. (Mimeo.)

(6)   Kagan, Jerome, and others. "Personality and IQ Change." *Journal of Abnormal and Social Psychology* 56: 261-66; March 1958.

(7)   Peters, H. J. "Counseling Services for Talented High School Students." *Working with Superior Students: Theories and Practices*. (Edited by Bruce Shertzer.) Chicago: Science Research Associates, 1960. p. 201-208.

(8)   Social Security Administration, Children's Bureau. *Your Gifted Child*. Bulletin No. 371. Washington, D. C.: Superintendent of Documents, Government Printing Office, 1959. 39 p.

(9)   Sontag, L. W., and others. "Mental Growth and Personality Development." *Social Research and Child Development*, Vol. 1, No. 68. Lafayette, Ind.: Purdue University, Child Development Publications, 1958.

(10)   Terman, L. M., and others. *The Gifted Child Grows Up*. Genetic Studies of Genius, Vol. 4. Stanford, Calif.: Stanford University Press, 1947. 448 p.

CHAPTER V

Responsibilities of the Guidance Counselor in Research

Research and evaluation are essential aspects of any good guidance program. They play a particularly important role in the guidance of the academically talented. Any school which attempts to meet the needs of talented students finds itself faced with major decisions regarding individualism,* grouping, acceleration, enrichment, programs of study—and the effectiveness of the decisions must be determined.

Research, as it is understood by research specialists, can rarely be undertaken by guidance counselors because of limitations imposed by pressures of other duties, lack of adequate clerical help, lack of money, and insufficient training in research design and techniques. There are, however, many activities of a research nature which can and should be undertaken. These activities may not deserve the title of research, yet they can be of great importance in determining the success of a local program for the academically talented. Furthermore, they should be undertaken because they are activities for which the guidance counselor must feel a special responsibility. If he does not assume the responsibility, it is unlikely that the administrator or the classroom teacher will be able to do so.

These activities of a research nature are concerned mainly with the accumulation of data and the presentation and interpretation of the data to those who are responsible for planning and conducting special programs for the academically talented. If their decisions are to be sound, administrators need all the informa-

---

* MacCurdy, R. D. "Individualism for the Gifted Child." *Phi Delta Kappan* 41:408-409; June 1960.

tion that can be made available. The guidance counselor, because of his familiarity with cumulative records, test administration and interpretation, and counseling procedures, is the logical person to supply most of the information.

It is the responsibility of the counselor to recommend suitable criteria for the selection of students for special programs. It is his responsibility, also, by means of follow-up procedures, to determine the effectiveness of the selection procedures and to decide whether any modification is needed. Evaluation of this sort must be classified as a kind of research activity. The results may be of limited use elsewhere, but they are vital to the success of the local program.

Selection procedures may be successful from the point of view of immediate academic success, but may impose undesirable pressures on certain students and have unfortunate repercussions later. It is the responsibility of the counselor to use all the available techniques at his disposal to determine whether any individual student is suffering harm from the program. The counselor, in reaching his conclusion, must engage in activity of a research nature. His findings may not permit generalization, but they are most important in his own school.

Follow-up studies to determine the success, or lack of success, of high-school graduates in higher education or in the employment of their choice, are an accepted part of any good guidance program. With the academically talented, such follow-up studies are of particular significance. The mere gathering of information is not research, no matter how carefully done, but as soon as the counselor begins to use the information to evaluate the success of the school's program for the academically talented, his work begins to verge on research. Follow-up studies of graduates are long-range efforts which do not produce immediate results, but the results, when produced, are very much worthwhile. Furthermore, the school, unlike the university or state department of education, is in a good position to conduct this particular kind of research activity.

Guidance counselors may participate in research projects that extend beyond their own schools. It is essential, of course, that such projects be designed and directed by research specialists, such as the school psychologist. If time is available, the school counselor can render able assistance to a district-wide, county-wide, or state-wide program. By participating, he not only will gain experience in research and an understanding of its role; he will also have the satisfaction of knowing that he is helping to advance the cause of knowledge. There are still many unanswered questions about the education of the academically talented. There is an obvious need for broad programs of research, as well as for research activity to meet local needs. The school counselor's primary responsibility in the research field is to supply the local administrative authorities with the information they need to enable them to solve local problems. Participation in outside projects is not the counselor's first responsibility and must always be on a voluntary basis and to the extent that his other duties permit. Participation is, nevertheless, highly desirable because of the opportunity it gives to the counselor to extend his own field of knowledge and, thereby, increase his own effectiveness.

The counselor who has had specialized training in research techniques will undoubtedly wish to go beyond the research activities which have been mentioned so far, and which may be considered the responsibility of any counselor. The extent to which the counselor will be able to engage in genuine research activities will be determined, of course, by the limitations of time, energy, and money, but it is to be hoped that school administrators fortunate enough to have research-trained counselors available, will take full advantage of their services. The provision of extra clerical help and a modest appropriation in the budget may enable such a coun-

selor to provide invaluable information to the administrator. True research at the local level is possible in
in many communities if administrators provide encouragement and support.

TRENDS OF RESEARCH

All areas of knowledge are enlarging and becoming
more complex. Research concerned with gifted young
people and relevant for counselors shows a similar trend.
New educational and psychological research tends to
investigate many aspects of the individual and to describe him from many points of view. It simultaneously
looks at the learning situation in a multifaceted way.
These complex individuals and complex situations are
then studied together, e.g., how does the creative, lower-
class, male child fare when placed with the rigid,
middle-class, female teacher? The old tunnel-vision way
of looking at slices of children and wedges of environment is considered inadequate. The counselor of the
future will find answers to intricate placement and adjustment problems in research that begins to approach
the complexity of real life.

These new trends in research apply particularly to the
gifted. Government (HEW, NIMH, NSF) and foundation (Ford, Carnegie, Rockefeller, Stern) research funds
are typically supporting multivariable (complex) inves-
tigations which are often particularly concerned with
the academically talented student. Large school systems
—both city and county—and state programs (e.g., New
York and California) show similar concerns. More often
than not, these studies are done by a team of workers—
counselor, teacher, sociologist, psychologist, and statis-
tician—a multivariate study by a multidiscipline team.
Some of the inadequacies of early studies, such as the
sociologist's failure to include intelligence test results
and the psychologist's lack of concern for social class,
are avoided when an interdisciplinary approach is used.

There is, then, a movement away from overly simplified and narrowly defined research. Classical psychological research on a single variable, as well as large-scale sociological research of the survey and tabulation type, have both tended to neglect too much of the sequence and context of situations and thus cannot be said to adequately represent the actions and conditions of life.* A most elementary caution is that results (difference between means) worth noting should be reported in terms of significant differences. Educational literature is replete with studies which lead the reader to believe results are noteworthy, when these untested differences could easily have occurred by chance.

In the multidimensional study of the individual, the following variables are frequently investigated:

1. Sex
2. Age
3. Level of intelligence
4. Achievement (objective test) data
5. Marks (grade point average)
6. Aspiration level (present occupation choice)
7. Socioeconomic status
   a. father and mother education
   b. occupation
8. Other cultural factors
   a. ethnic (cross-national and cross-cultural research)
   b. religious
9. Attitudes—Values
   a. open mind versus closed mind, dogmatism
   b. tolerance versus authoritarianism

---

* Classical research studies, where all the variables are controlled but one, are no longer considered satisfactory. Nor is the artificial environment of the laboratory considered a suitable locale for studying people. It is hard to control the situation in the laboratory, and when it is controlled, it is difficult to apply the findings to other situations such as the classroom. Needless to say, any reported findings must be accepted with caution when situations are of the unnatural, laboratory type or when too few aspects of the situation or characteristics of the individual are investigated.

  c. creativeness verses conformity
  d. responsibility
  e. self-concept
  f. achievement motivation
10. Developmental level (task, stage) studies

A multivariate view of the situation might include:
1. Teachers' characteristics
  a. authoritarian versus democratic
  b. cold versus warm
  c. threatening versus accepting
2. Teaching methods and approaches
  a. textbook and recitation
  b. research and problem solving
  c. group discussions
  d. independent study
  e. teaching machines
3. Administrative provisions
  a. track systems and grouping
  b. acceleration
  c. guidance program
4. Types of material
  a. texts
  b. reference books
  c. audio-visual materials
  d. laboratory supplies
5. Subject areas (mathematics, English, science, language, etc.)

New areas are being investigated. There is less emphasis on sensory-motor testing than before World War II (the traditional theory that intelligence would be related to sensory acuity is no longer held), a broadening of the intelligence test (multifactor approaches),* and an ever-growing concern with nonintellectual factors such as personality development.

Projective techniques supplement the paper-and-pencil personality inventories. New positive-dimension per-

---

* Verbal, spatial, perceptual, memory, and reasoning factors.

sonality tests measure responsibility, self-confidence, autonomy, etc., instead of measuring only abnormal dimensions such as paranoia and anxiety. Added to these are measures of authoritarianism and dogmatism, creativity, critical thinking, and the self-concept. Indexes of social status, sociometric instruments, and tools to investigate leadership also have been developed. Much interest is being shown in the experiments and speculations relating to motivation. Group dynamics, the cause-effect changes within a social group, is another new and flourishing study area. Tape recordings, filmed records, and trained observers are used to record salient aspects of group work. There have been great advances made in opinion polling, questionnaire construction, and sampling techniques. Complex statistical approaches (such as analysis of variance, covariance, and factor analysis) and electronic calculators (at least 100 universities now have computers) make it possible to deal with this welter of results, or perhaps the possibilities of handling the figures mathematically have encouraged the collection of these masses of data.

However, it must be pointed out that the machines can calculate answers faster than tests can be given and data collected. Thus, counselors and other school people are faced not only with a burgeoning population (students, ad infinitum) but also a research explosion. Knowledge about superior young people—where they come from, and how and where they may flourish—will undoubtedly soon exceed the capacities of teachers to scan and absorb such knowledge. The lag between "what we know" and "what we do" may easily increase if counselors cannot perform two important functions:

1. Know more, on the one hand, about the talented student and his needs and, on the other hand, be wise enough to counsel well and guide appropriately. This means that reading research studies (descriptions of students and their needs, and reports of programs and their functioning), is a vital part of the counselor's task.

This is part of the counselor's "homework." It also means that the counselor should collect and use data on his counselees. Too often information about the student is never adequately and systematically collected, or if collected, it is allowed to lie fallow in a filing cabinet. Similarly, information about students-at-large and school programs remains unscanned in the periodicals.

2. Serve as liaison persons in presenting and interpreting material to the teachers who often do not have the skills to do original research or the time to keep abreast of the literature. The counselor then must be a translator for school personnel as well as make use of research findings in his own work.

CURRENT RESEARCH TELLS THE GUIDANCE WORKER ABOUT THE ACADEMICALLY TALENTED

As consumers of research, it is important for the guidance worker to evaluate critically all research findings and avoid overgeneralizing from the data. An attempt has been made to support the generalizations made in the following pages. It is hoped that the reader will examine these sources before accepting them as "truth."

Research tells us that the academically talented show their abilities early in life and accomplish their best work between the ages of 25 and 40.

Dennis, Wayne. "Age and Achievement: A Critique." *Journal of Gerontology* 11:331-33; July 1956.
Dennis, Wayne. "The Age Decrement in Outstanding Scientific Contributions: Fact or Artifact?" *American Psychologist* 13:457-60; August 1958.
Lehman, Harvey C. *Age and Achievement.* Princeton, N.J.: Princeton University Press, 1953. 358 p.
Terman, L. M. "The Discovery and Encouragement of Exceptional Talent." *American Psychologist* 9:221-30; June 1954.
Terman, L. M., and Oden, Melita H. *The Gifted Child Grows Up.* Stanford, Calif.: Stanford University Press, 1947. p. 28.
Worcester, D. A. *The Education of Children of Above Average Mentality.* Lincoln: University of Nebraska Press, 1956. 68 p.

Research tells us that the academically talented do well emotionally, socially, and academically when admitted to school earlier than the rest of the population and do well when accelerated.

Flesher, Marie A. "Did They Graduate Too Young?" *Educational Research Bulletin* 24:218-21; November 1945.

Holmes, Jack A., and Finley, Carmen J. "Underage and Overage Grade Placements and School Achievement." *Journal of Educational Psychology* 48:447-56; November 1957.

Pressey, S. L. *Educational Acceleration: Appraisals and Basic Problems.* Columbus: Ohio State University, 1949. 153 p.

Pressey, S. L., and Combs, Arthur. "Acceleration and Age of Productivity." *Educational Research Bulletin* 22:191-96; October 1943.

Terman, L. M. "Discovery and Encouragement of Exceptional Talent." *American Psychologist* 9:221-30; June 1954.

Research tells us that a high percentage of academically talented students do not attend college. These sources describe the influence of guidance programs in decreasing this number and reasons why the percentage is so high.

Carter, W. R. "University Students Are Getting Better Every Year!" *Vocational Guidance Quarterly* 6:171-73; Summer 1958.

Rummell, F. V., and Johnson, C. M. "Bill Lane's Students Win Prizes." *Reader's Digest* 66:29-32; January 1955.

Toops, H. "The Prediction of College-Going." *School and Society* 51:257-61; March 1940.

Wolfle, D. *America's Resources of Specialized Talent.* New York: Harper & Brothers, 1954. p. 251.

Research tells us about the status of programs for the academically talented that have been in existence for a long enough period of time to allow for some evaluation.

Andree, R. G., and Master, M. "What Are Some Promising Programs for Gifted Students?" Summary of Presentations. *National Association of Secondary-School Principals Bulletin* 38:314-23; April 1954.

Barbe, Walter B. "Evaluation of Special Classes for Gifted Children." *Exceptional Children* 22:60-62; November 1955.

Barbe, Walter B., and Norris, Dorothy E. "Special Classes for Gifted Children in Cleveland." *Exceptional Children* 21:55-57; November 1954.

Brumbaugh, Florence N. "Our Youngest Intellectuals Thirteen Years Later." *Exceptional Children* 21:168-70; February 1955.

Dunlap, James M. "Gifted Children in an Enriched Program." *Exceptional Children* 21:135-37; January 1955.

The London Times. "New York School for Geniuses." *London Times Educational Supplement*, May 13, 1960. p. 966-67.

Morhous, Francis E., and Sherley, Elizabeth. "A High School Program for Gifted Students." *School Executive* 75:39-44; July 1956.

Pregler, Hedwig. "The Colfax Plan." *Exceptional Children* 20:198-201; February 1954.

Wilson, Frank. "Some Special Ability Test Scores of Gifted Children." *Journal of Genetic Psychology* 82:59-68; March 1953.

Research tells us that a special kind of teacher is needed for the academically talented.

Barbe, Walter B., and Norris, Dorothy E. "Special Classes for Gifted Children in Cleveland." *Exceptional Children* 21:55-57; November 1954.

Davis, Nelda. "Teachers for the Gifted." *Journal of Teacher Education* 5:221-24; September 1954.

Mackie, Romaine, and Dunn, Lloyd. "State Standards for Teaching Our Nation's 5,000,000 Exceptional Children." *Journal of Teacher Education* 4:271-74; December 1953.

Wilson, Frank T. "In-Service and Undergraduate Preparation of Teachers of the Gifted." *Educational Administration and Supervision* 43:295-301; May 1957.

Wilson, Frank T. "The Preparation of Teachers for the Education of Gifted Children." *Education for the Gifted.* Fifty-Seventh Yearbook, Part II, National Society for the Study of Education. Chicago: University of Chicago Press, 1958. Chapter 15, p. 362-76.

Research tells us that accelerated academically talented students appear to be as personally and socially adjusted as other students.

Gallagher, James J., and Crowder, Thora H. "Adjustment of Gifted Children in the Regular Classroom." *Exceptional Children* 23:306-12; April 1957.

Justman, Joseph. "Personal and Social Adjustment of Intellectually Gifted Accelerants and Non-accelerants in Junior High School." *School Review* 61:468-78; November 1953.

Keys, Noel. "Adjustment of Under-age Students in High School." *Psychological Bulletin* 32:539; October 1935.

Miller, Robert V. "Social Status and Sociometric Differences Among Mentally Superior, Mentally Typical, and Mentally Retarded Children." *Exceptional Children* 23:114-19; December 1956.

Pressey, S. L. "Age of College Graduation and Success in Adult Life." *Journal of Applied Psychology* 30:226-33; June 1946.

Pressey, S. L. *Educational Acceleration: Appraisals and Basic Problems.* Columbus: Ohio State University, 1949. 153 p.

Shannon, Dan C. "What Research Says About Acceleration." *Phi Delta Kappan* 39:70-72; November 1957.

Terman, L. M. "Discovery and Encouragement of Exceptional Talent." *American Psychologist* 9:221-30; June 1954.